THUNDER

IN THE SOUTHWEST

Echoes from the Wild Frontier

BY

Oren Arnold

WITH DRAWINGS BY NICK EGGENHOFER

UNIVERSITY OF OKLAHOMA PRESS

NORMAN

BY OREN ARNOLD:
Wild Americans (Chicago, 1937)
Roundup (Dallas, 1937)
Hot Irons (New York, 1940)
Savage Son (Albuquerque, 1951)
Thunder in the Southwest (Norman, 1952)
and others

Copyright 1952 by the University of Oklahoma Press
Publishing Division of the University
Composed and printed at Norman, Oklahoma, U.S.A.
by the University of Oklahoma Press
First Edition

To a Southwestern Man-Among-Men
Dewey W. Swihart

ACKNOWLEDGMENTS

FOR ABOUT one hundred years book and magazine editors have served us a steady diet of "wild western" stories, and we love it today more than ever. So far as I can learn, no harm whatsoever has come from this, though a few self-appointed "literary" critics have worried and wondered. They get confused when we point out that the *facts* of western history are wilder than any yarns the fictioneers can concoct—which is the fundamental premise of this volume. Many distinguished and scholarly folk have loved "detective stories" and "westerns" such as these, notably Presidents Theodore Roosevelt, William Howard Taft, Woodrow Wilson, and Franklin Delano Roosevelt, who enjoyed them without attaching undue importance to them. Some of my most exciting episodes were tested on such audiences years ago in magazines, apparently to the delight of all. I still get heartening fan mail about pieces published in the nineteen thirties and early nineteen forties. I am grateful to my magazine editor friends for allowing me to enlarge and adapt some of my articles for more permanent presentation here. The amazing account of "Doc and Kate, The First Stage Robbers," for instance, is adapted by courtesy of *True*, the Man's Magazine (copyright 1944, Fawcett Publications, Inc.); "Clover in the Coffin" from an article by the same title by courtesy of *Startling Detective Magazine* (copyright 1946, Fawcett Publications, Inc.). Other journals that have graciously allowed me to draw on my own writings

vii

include *Coronet, The Saturday Evening Post, Pageant, Real Detective, Startling Detective, Inside Detective, Sensation, Magazine Digest, Desert Magazine, American Forests,* and *Family Circle.* Pioneer families, historians, and others have added much for use in the book, and my thanks go to all.

OREN ARNOLD

Phoenix, Arizona

CONTENTS

THUNDER IN THE SOUTHWEST
Echoes from the Wild Frontier

PROLOGUE

THIS IS NOT a work of fiction, nor is it a "history" in the conventional sense. It is a re-enactment of certain episodes which took place in the Southwest that our pioneers knew.

Use has been made of subject and treatment calculated to arouse excited interest and emotional response, a melodramatic styling known to some as sensationalism. *Why* is it styled so? Because a great segment of our people prefer it that way, and they are the majority. They, not the few who affect a certain literary dilettantism, or even the few who are genuine scholars, represent America. Moreover, they are the same type of folk as those who lived these episodes.

Accounts of some of the adventures related here appear only piecemeal in the formal histories, and some can never be documented at all, because in those harried times people could not pause to set down much about the events taking place around them. But the Southwest is still young: since I began these tales in 1920 I have talked to many of the actual participants. From them and from eyewitnesses I have obtained the wealth of detail, then put it together the way *they* liked to do. Where there were discrepancies in their reports, I have taken the logical course and used the version most likely to be entertaining.

Accept the book, then, for what it is meant to be—a happy, hybrid combination of fact and folklore.

2

1

BLACK GHOSTS OF BISBEE

WHEN a woman screams, the high-pitched sound is arresting enough. But when a man screams it is more than alarming; abject terror grips everybody within earshot.

Mrs. Anna Roberts shrieked first, on this normally quiet street at Bisbee, Arizona. Her outcry was punctuated by the bark of a gun. Mrs. Roberts fell moaning, dying.

A moment later the man screamed. He was three tiers of houses—some 80 feet—above the main street and the sidewalks, for Bisbee's narrow canyons make this a stair-step town. He had heard the hullabaloo and perhaps had sensed the tragedy and danger in a way some people have. He had come out on his front porch, and—*Bang!* Again that bark from a gun. Pain and death itself struck him, toppled him off the porch, and sent him bumping, rolling, tumbling, screaming down the steep incline. By the time he struck the lower level pavement he, too, was quite dead. His name, we are told, was Dave Rousseau.

The populace in crowded little Bisbee, a mining camp, heard the shots and outcries. In a matter of seconds another staccato of gunfire echoed and re-echoed in the rock canyons, off the store buildings, and around the clustered homes. Doors slammed. People shouted. Men came running. Horses' hoofs beat a wild drumming down the pavement and into the flat valley, then faded away.

3

"It's at the G-C Store, the G-C Store!" someone yelled. "Where's Doctor King? And Tom Smith?"

"Oh, my God! My God in Heaven!"

A note of horror swept the village now as people gathered quickly. J. C. Kriegbaum, an honored citizen, was standing there, holding his gun and crying over his dead friend. "Dad" Goldwater paced up and down. Señor Casteñeda was shrieking for an officer and R. E. Duvall stood in a daze clutching his neck while blood strained through his fingers.

It was J. C. Kriegbaum who finally regained enough poise to take charge. In half an hour, five bodies were resting on the porch of the Goldwater and Casteñeda store. They were the remains of Mrs. Roberts, Mr. Rousseau, J. D. Tapner, Albert Nolly, and Tom Smith, the last a deputy sheriff. Night had fully blackened the canyon now, so at least the visual horror was dimmed as people listened to what had occurred.

Messrs. Goldwater and Casteñeda had been counting their day's receipts in the little office at the back of their store. In a rich mining town the money was considerable, and there was more in the open safe. The total cash exceeded $30,000. Clerks were busy straightening the merchandise, and only one customer was inside, R. E. Duvall, who was being fitted with a pair of shoes. All at once the front door burst open. Two black-hooded men stood there, holding guns.

"Put all the money in a bag, Goldwater!" one bandit ordered. "Get that out of the safe. The rest of you—stand still!"

It was at about this moment that Mrs. Anna Roberts screamed outside. She had seen the two bandits enter the store, and she saw four more masked men waiting on the

4

front porch. The shot that killed her was echoed inside by the shot that struck Duvall. He did not "freeze," as ordered; he had reached for his gun.

One bandit walked back to be sure all the money was sacked. He made Goldwater tie the cloth bag. Then he paused at a showcase of jewelry.

Crash! . . . *Crash!* He swung one pistol through the showcase glass, slipped the gun in its holster, and with his free hand pocketed some of the rings and two of the fanciest watches. This delayed him several seconds, during which time the fanfare of guns was roaring outside.

On the street, each person who appeared was shot at. But for the dimming twilight not just five but a dozen or more would surely have been killed, for the bandits cracked down at everything that moved, giving no warning and saying few words. Before anybody could fully realize what was happening, the six raiders had run to their horses and galloped away.

With Tom Smith, the deputy sheriff, killed, Mr. Kriegbaum told the frantic people that he would carry the news to the county seat. Then he dashed away. The horse he rode was a good one, but the route he had to travel was rough and dangerous and extended more than thirty miles. Mr. Kriegbaum made that run in barely two hours—his horse died from the strain of it—and in short order three deputies were leading an armed force back to Bisbee. The three leaders were John Behan, Robert Paul, and W. L. Daniels. At least two of those had already achieved renown, for this was in the wild-western year of 1883 and the county-seat town, which was headquarters, was named Tombstone. John Behan had become sheriff there, an office he held during the famed Earp-Clanton feud, and Bob Paul had won distinction as shotgun messenger on the Wells Fargo stage. In

5

the Bisbee massacre, however, Behan and Paul became detectives whose work has not been exceeded in all the history
of the West.

"There ain't a thing to go on, gentlemen!" Mr. Goldwater told them, when the posse from Tombstone arrived.
"Absolutely not a thing! Six men on six horses is all we
know. It was nigh dark, and they all wore black stockings
over their heads."

Bob Paul, a stolid, heavy man, sat on his horse in front of
the posse, listening.

"Not one identified, eh?" he questioned, quietly. "No
clues."

"Not a thing, Mr. Paul. Nobody could tell who they
might've been. With them stockings covering their heads,
they just looked like black ghosts!"

Women near him sobbed and wailed, while men stood
waiting with their loaded guns.

"The time will come," promised the deputy at last,
"when those murderers will wear black stockings again.
And be black ghosts forever."

It was an official vow of vengeance, but little could be
done immediately. Mr. Paul and Mr. Behan went over every
detail of the raid and murders and took notes about the
money, and bag used, the rings, the watches, and the descriptions of the hooded men, while Mr. Daniels saw that
the possemen were equipped with fresh horses and canteens
of water. John Heath appeared during these activities.
Heath was a comparative stranger in town, who said that
he knew all the trails in this part of Arizona Territory and
all the water holes. He would be glad to serve as guide for
the posse, he told Mr. Paul.

No other guide was available on such short notice, so
Heath's offer was accepted. The men rode out shortly before midnight. They had to move slowly because of dark-

ness; but Heath, leading them, kept a sharp eye on the ground.

"I don't quite make out all you say you see, Heath," Bob Paul told the man frankly.

"Takes an experienced trailer," Heath countered. "Lots of traffic been criss-crossing here, sheriff. Cattle, ranchers, ore hauling. But I believe the tracks left by them six bandits is plain."

The posse took his word for it and rode hard in the direction he indicated. The men reasoned that the bandits must have been drinking heavily to have shot down people in cold blood as they had, so they might have a false sense of security and stop soon for rest and celebration. Or, if they did not, the trail would be more easily followed by daylight.

At dawn, though, the man Heath was crestfallen. When Deputy Paul pinned him down Heath admitted that he had lost the trail. There had been a rocky stretch several miles long. Somewhere back there the criminals must have slipped off, perhaps one by one so that tracks would escape the attention of any who followed. Disappointed and angry, the possemen turned back.

Before noon Heath was elated again.

"This here's it!" he cried, coming onto tracks of horses. "I knowed we'd pick it up. We wouldn't have missed it in daylight!"

They felt that maybe his alibi was sound. They rode behind him a long way and by noon were fatigued with their riding. Part of the trail had passed over rocky land again, some of it along "cattle runs," but of course this was the sort of trick the fleeing men would naturally use. It was well after noon, while the posse was resting, that Deputies Paul and Behan again confronted John Heath.

"I have to admit," he confessed after long questioning, "I ain't none too sure of it again."

7

"Why didn't you tell us!" Paul demanded. Other men stood up angrily.

"I can make a big circle by myself while you men wait here," Heath offered. "When I find it again, I'll come git you. It's all I know to do."

The anger against Heath was strong now. Had the posse been led deliberately on a wild goose chase? Paul and Behan told him that for his own safety he'd better head back to Bisbee alone.

Three days later the riders straggled back, completely whipped. Not a sign of the murderers had been found. No clue worthy of the name had been unearthed. The funerals had been held, and the town was in despair when it learned of the posse's failure. John Heath was dejected and ashamed, though people decided that his disgrace might not be altogether merited. But deputies Paul and Behan were deter-

mined to stay on the job. They elected to move henceforth as quietly as they could, unattended by a clattering posse.

Working as a pair, the two men began to ride from day to day about the countryside. Even risking the attacks of savage Apache Indians, who were still scattered through southern Arizona, the two men went far to the outlying ranches, replenishing their supplies as they traveled, making little noise but sticking to their job.

"It stands to reason," John Behan said one day, "that the bandits would have to see somebody some time, to get grub if nothing else. It would be so much easier if we only knew who they were!"

As if in answer to that prayer, the names of the bandits were learned about twenty-four hours later. Behan and Paul had ridden out again and had stopped for the night at the Frank Buckles ranch.

"You're more than welcome," the family assured him. "Come in and tell us the news. We ain't seen nobody since Heath and his men stopped two, three weeks ago. We git hungry for news of what's—"

"Who?" Bob Paul spoke, but both officers had perked up.

"Why, John Heath. Him and some men stopped." Frank Buckles said. "I sold 'em four horses, in fact. But I demanded cash money. I don't like the crowd he was with. You take Comer Sample, that redhead. And that Dan Dowd. And Jack Howard. They're cattle thieves as shore as the sun sets! Only we ranchers ain't been able to prove it."

"Heath come with them!"

"Why, yes. Why?"

They told the rancher what had happened in Bisbee and related the failure of the posse guided by Heath.

"Dowd is suspected of attacking the Benson stage out of Tombstone," Paul declared. "We caught one of a band

9

that tried a holdup, and he named Dowd. Who else come here, Mr. Buckles?"

The rancher gave careful thought. "Near as I can remember, there was one named Vaughn, a man named Dan Kelly, and another one, Delancy, or something like that. I wouldn't trust one of them ten feet!"

The deputies asked for all the available details, and finally Mr. Buckles said, "What do you make of it?"

"I think we may have something," Bob Paul answered. "Behan, you stay out here and begin to ride among the friendly Mexicans and Indians. Take plenty of little gifts along, and some good hard silver money. Make your plans careful. Understand?"

"I understand. What do you aim to do, Bob?"

"I'm going in to town and arrest John Heath."

When Paul returned to Bisbee he conferred with the third deputy, Mr. Daniels. Together they went to Heath on a street corner, two armed men approaching from two directions. Paul held a cocked pistol. He had planned some artistic bluffing.

"It's all up, Heath," said he. "Don't try to draw. We'll kill you in two seconds. We know who it was, and we know you was one of them."

Heath tried bluffing, but a gun muzzle touched his ribs. He blustered indignantly.

"No good, Heath," Paul went on. "Your pal Dowd talked. So did Red Sample. You were left here to keep an eye on us, you thought; but really you were left here holding the bag!"

The next instant handcuffs clicked on Heath, and he began swearing in a burst of fury. It was what the deputies wanted. In his anger he verified what they had thought: Dan Dowd, Red Sample, Jack Howard, Bill Delaney (not Delancy), Daniel Kelly, and Jim Vaughn were the six murderers who had robbed the Goldwater and Casteñeda store and left five citizens dead and one wounded on that evening nearly three weeks ago. John Heath had been a front man for them, a blind—and a bag-holder indeed!

To save Heath from lynching the officers slipped him away to Tombstone. Deputy Daniels went on an official tour of the territory, quietly spreading a description of the wanted men and offering rewards for their capture. And because "the Dan Dowd gang" of suspected cattle thieves were already fairly well known, clues began to pop up again and again. Deputies Behan and Paul assiduously followed them up.

A government surveyor, traveling through from northern Arizona, happened to remember seeing a cowboy who answered Jim Vaughn's description. In a village saloon this man had scattered money right and left—a sure sign, because cowboys didn't have much money. Bob Paul went the more than three hundred miles by stage to the town.

In such a small village Paul's arrival couldn't be missed, and Vaughn instantly spotted him. Proof of Vaughn's guilt came when he quickly fled. He first took refuge from the relentless deputy in the office of a small sawmill, and because Vaughn had been among friends—of a sort—up here, Deputy Paul could get no one to help go after the criminal. So he elected to go alone.

The office was situated in the usual clearing near the mill, and to approach it openly would have meant sure death, Paul knew. Therefore, he worked out a plan. The sawmill had been handling some hardwood timber. Mr. Paul got a heavy oak slab two inches thick, eighteen inches wide, and about five feet long. He nailed a handle to this, then holding it in his left hand and like a shield such as savages used, the courageous deputy walked toward the wooden shack with a cocked pistol in his right hand.

"Come out of it hands up, Vaughn!" he ordered. "I'm going to take you dead or alive!"

Pow! Vaughn shot first. Paul answered him, aiming at a window pane, the only target he could see. The next moment Deputy Paul discovered that courage alone is not enough to win battles, not even when it is reinforced with an oak board. Vaughn shot once more, this time with a rifle. The bullet did what a pistol slug couldn't have done: it tore through the oak shield, struck Paul's left holster and pistol, spun him around, and made him fall. He lay there, momentarily dazed, a perfect target now.

But Vaughn evidently thought he had already killed him, and fearful of another murder on his head, he ran from the rear of the house and took to the hills. In a moment Paul got up and ran for his horse.

The man-for-man chase lasted then for six and a half days. Vaughn led Paul out of the forest land and into the painted deserts and vermilion-cliff country. Paul strained every ounce of muscle and nerve to travel by night as well as by day. Occasionally he sighted his man at a distance. He stalked him at night, hoping to see a campfire or a movement that would reveal Vaughn's location. But the outlaw was too shrewd. Paul bought fresh horses from Navajo Indians in order to travel faster. From a study of the tracks he knew that Vaughn had done the same thing.

On two occasions Paul lost the trail completely. The first time this happened, distressed about it for hours, he finally caught a distant glimpse of antelope stampeding.

"He's trying to kill food!" Paul exulted and headed that direction. He saw no dead antelope but found the remains of a hasty camp and the tracks of Vaughn's horse.

The second time he lost the trail, Bob Paul saw buzzards circling. On the off-chance of being lucky again he went to that spot and found the remains of a horse from which meat had been taken. Jim Vaughn had been desperate for food! The deputy pressed on.

The showdown came at the base of Houserock, a landmark now made famous by a wild buffalo herd that roams there under state protection. Vaughn, frantic, set a trap. He commandeered an Indian boy who could speak English. Staying in ambush himself, he sent the Indian out under threat of death to speak with the officer and lead him, unsuspecting, within rifle range. The scheme worked.

"Is white man, dead," the Indian said to Bob Paul. "Is blood."

"Where?" Paul demanded.

"Up there, in rocks. You come."

Paul went closer. So he had wounded Vaughn, and Vaughn had finally died. Well and good. He would go see about the remains.

Crack! Outdoors this time, the rifle report was sharper. Vaughn shot from behind a rock. Paul, struck in the chest, fell backwards downhill.

That was the closest Jim Vaughn ever came to being arrested for the Bisbee murders, for even though he was subsequently trailed and chased again, officers never got in sight of him. Before they could finally close in, Vaughn took part in a raid at the frontier village of St. Johns. There he was shot dead in a street battle.

Fortunately, Deputy Paul's wound was not serious. The Indian boy carried him to a hogan, and other Indians brought the white government agent. Within a few weeks Paul was back in Bisbee virtually a well man, though a disappointed one.

But he had no time to rest. His fellow deputies had other hot clues. Mr. Behan was back from a long trip that included every town of any size along the Arizona-New Mexico line, and it was from one of these, Clifton, Arizona, that the next clue came. In Clifton as elsewhere Mr. Behan had spread his descriptions of the wanted men. He told of the money stolen and of the jewelry taken from the Goldwater and Casteñeda store. One stolen watch could be described in detail. It had fine works and several diamonds in the case.

In Clifton a young miner named Pickering was courting a local girl. On one particular night she acted anything but cordial to him, and it developed that a new man in town had stolen Pickering's play. The girl taunted Pickering with being stingy.

"George gives me the ni-i-i-cest things!" she declared, referring to the new man. "If you don't believe me, look at this."

Pickering looked at her exhibit. It included a valuable ring and a gemmed watch! And Pickering had chanced to hear Deputy Behan's conversation some two weeks before.

"Where's this George from?" he demanded.

"Never mind. You're just jealous."

"Maybe I am, maybe I am."

Pickering then left the girl and looked up his rival, who claimed his name was George Lincoln and who was eternally to be seen in the company of another rather swaggering gent. Pickering could learn nothing about them except that they claimed to have come from the East. They didn't look like easterners to Pickering. He sent a message down to Deputy Behan in Tombstone, but it was Bob Paul who quietly came in to Clifton and sought out Pickering.

"Your description sounds right," Paul admitted. "Red hair, weighs about 200. His friend kinky-headed and not so good looking. Older man prob'ly, eh?"

"That's them!" Pickering was excited. "You going to arrest them?"

"We'll see. Show me where they're at."

Mr. Paul first saw the fugitives as they were taking a

14

two-seated surrey from a corral. He watched them ride away, then rented a horse for himself and set out to follow.

"Ain't you going to have a posse?" Pickering asked.

"Tried that once," Paul answered dryly. "Didn't work."

The surrey stopped at a "hotel" and picked up two girls. Paul loitered inconspicuously behind, chinning casually with ore-wagon drivers. When he saw that the two couples were heading up the Yellow Canyon road, a beautiful drive, he cut behind a slag dump and a row of shacks, spurred his horse, and got well ahead of the surrey. Then, like a bandit himself, Deputy Paul waited behind the screen of some oak shrubbery.

When the surrey came near, the loving in the seats had already become rather passionate. Paul was within arm's reach before they saw him. But he was recognized at once.

"Howard! Sample! I'll blow you both to hell if you make one move!"

Red Sample literally threw his girl across the dashboard in scrambling to get his gun.

Bang! Bang! Paul shot him twice, miraculously not killing him.

Both girls screamed in terror, and Jack Howard threw up his hands.

"Don't shoot me, don't shoot!" he begged.

Red Sample, moaning and bleeding, had slumped over inert. The surrey horses began to plunge; terrified by the screaming and the shots, they were about to stampede. Paul was forced to kill one of them. Then with a gun at Howard's back he disarmed the man and handcuffed him.

A week later the two outlaws were on their way to Tombstone, Sample on a stretcher but nowhere near dead. The two met John Heath in jail. The black ghosts of Bisbee were having a reunion.

While Paul was operating at Clifton, Behan and Daniels

15

cashed in on friendly seed sown among humble folk. Mexican families, like Indians, had a way of sending word-of-mouth news through all their clan. Men, women, and children often connived to gather the most astonishing information in many devious ways, and the officers knew this. The good Mexican citizens of Bisbee had been as indignant as the Americans at the murderous raid. They were glad to help.

The deputies never learned exactly how the information chain had reached down into Chihuahua, Mexico, but one day Mr. Behan had a formal call from an elderly Mexican, one Constantino Monrovia.

"If she iss possible, Señor," Monrovia blandly suggested after several minutes of courteous small talk, "it might be well for you to make one trip to Sabinal, *sabe usted?*"

Mr. Behan swallowed. He had to think this through!

"You are wise, *amigo*," he told the older man. "Do you, then, advise my going there—uh—on official business, or maybe for my personal health?" Was somebody gunning for him here in Bisbee, and was he being warned, or—?

The guest was still formal. "It would not be my duty, nor am I able, to prescribe for a friend's health," said he.

"I believe I understand," Mr. Behan declared. "Shake hands."

The trip to Chihuahua was tedious but uneventful. Sabinal was a mining town. Behan posed, under an assumed name in rather flowery clothing, as an eastern buyer of smelted ore. But under his frock coat he carried two loaded pistols. The superintendent of the largest mine showed the visitor around in daytime, but at night the "Yankee" walked the noisy, dirty "liquor streets" alone. He had to use his reasoning at every turn. If one of the robbers were here, he told himself, the man would have money to spend and most likely would hang around the bars and gambling houses.

Again common sense—that weapon which all good officers of the law find invaluable—brought its reward to Mr. Behan. After scanning dozens of faces each night for more than a week of patient hunting, he peered through a saloon window one evening and suddenly discovered Dan Dowd.

He had known Dowd by sight up in Arizona. He did not mistake the man now, nor did he mistake the danger that would be involved in taking him. For one thing, this was a foreign land. A *gringo* or a Yankee officer arresting a man who spent money freely could easily get into trouble himself. So Behan took advantage of the night. He waited at a corner for Dowd to come past alone. Though he held a heavy pistol, he did not shoot it. As Dowd moved close— *whack!*

"Nn-n-n-n-n!" Dowd's knees buckled.

He groaned once more and then lay still. Behan pulled Dowd's limp form into the shadows, handcuffed and tied him, and in due time carried him in a rented wagon to a point near the international line. There, again operating at night so as to avoid the delay which extradition procedures might bring, he placed Dowd in an empty train boxcar and rode safely with him back to Arizona. Dowd went into jail with his henchmen at Tombstone.

Meanwhile, Bob Paul had also been active. Paul reasoned that if two of the bandits had traveled as far as Clifton, which was near the New Mexico border, others might also have fled in that direction. He resumed traveling, talking quietly, describing the wanted men, and offering rewards in every town and village. By this time news of the murders had spread everywhere, and all decent citizens were eager to help. Once again Paul's common-sense reasoning proved correct. One day while he was at Deming, New Mexico, a twelve-year-old Mexican shoeshine lad run up to him.

"Señor!" the lad was excited. "Is to come queek! *El barbero*, he send for you! You come!"

Paul hastened with him to a barbershop two blocks away. Four or five men stood nervously around. Augustín Salas, a fat Mexican barber, had a customer lying in his chair. Lather had been shaved off most of the man's face, but Salas stood over him threateningly with a long, keen razor at the man's throat.

"Señor Paul!" Salas greeted. "This man order shave. I cut off the much whiskers. I look at his face—Ha! 'You are Kellee!' I tell him. I feel muscles in his shoulder get tight. It is proof! 'Do not move!' I tell him. 'Me, I cut your throat— ha!' I send for you!"

"Good work, Salas!" Paul was astounded, but delighted as well. There indeed sat Daniel Kelly, sixth member of the Dan Dowd gang. Deputy Paul handcuffed him to the barber chair, disarmed him, and left him there until transportation back to Tombstone could be arranged. During the few hours that his shop served as an impromptu jail, Augustín Salas got more free advertising than he ever dreamed of. He refused any reward money, but the Mexican lad was given twenty dollars in gold.

Thus inexorably was the law closing down on the murderers who had raided Bisbee. Jim Vaughn had been shot down at St. Johns. Only one remained at large, Bill Delaney, and he was also traced through the "Mexican grapevine." Acting on this inside information, both Paul and Behan went to the Sonoran town of Minas Prietas. They took a friendly Mexican with them as interpreter and guide and waited with saddle horses on the edge of town while the Mexican took a message in to Delaney. Again, this procedure was necessary to avoid the possible complications of international law.

The Mexican messenger found the bandit without any trouble and approached him when he was alone.

"A friend wishes to see you, Señor Delaney," he spoke frankly.

Delaney the outlaw looked menacingly at the Mexican. "My name's Summers. You got the wrong man."

The Mexican smiled blandly. "Your friend, he is name Dowd. He say to tell you, Dan Dowd."

"Oh-h-h. That's different. Where is Dan?"

Half an hour later Bill Delaney, suspecting nothing, approached the saddled horses and called out rather eagerly, "Dan? You old son-of-a-gun, where are you?"

"Right here!" Deputy Paul answered, from his right.

"And right here!" Behan said, from the other side. "Better freeze in your tracks, Delaney!"

The Mexican had drawn a gun, too. Delaney could do nothing but swear violently. Five days later he was with Dan Dowd in reality, however, in the jail at Tombstone.

Trial of the outlaws now came swiftly. Feeling was very high. The criminals were identified beyond any question, and five of them were sentenced to be hanged. Since the sixth, John Heath, had not taken actual part in the murderous holdup, as Judge H. D. Penney told the jury, he was sentenced to life imprisonment. But Heath, too, was destined to stay with the Dan Dowd gang. Indignant citizens constituted a higher court and ruled that an informer and front man was as guilty as his henchmen, left Bisbee in a body, rode to Tombstone, and told the sheriff and all deputies to stand out of the way. Heath was taken out of jail screaming as Dave Rousseau had screamed on that fatal evening in Bisbee. Heath's screams ended when a rope strangled him as he was lifted, swinging, from the bar of a telegraph pole.

The Bisbee citizens were, however, content to wait for legal action on the other five criminals. The sheriff took at least nominal charge of that ceremony. He erected a scaffold that held not one but five gallows in a row, all controlled by one trap string. Hundreds of men and some women were at the scene at the appointed hour. A few, whose memories were keen, were sobbing. A priest said a few words, and a minister asked God's forgiveness. Sheriff John Ward adjusted five black hoods and five ropes. There was a minute or two filled with horrible noises.

The black ghosts of Bisbee had become black ghosts indeed.

2

NUMBER ONE BANDIT

DEPUTY SHERIFF Harrison was performing his official duty. "What am I bid? What am I bid?" he chanted, opening the auction. "Who'll start the bidding? . . . Ah, five dollars I am bid. . . . Five dollars. Five dollars. Do I hear ten?"

He heard ten. Then he heard fifteen, twenty, thirty.

But the bids came in peculiarly toneless voices. Each bidder in turn was scrutinized with interest by all the other onlookers. Standing before the auctioneer were two hundred more men and women, each of whom lacked the usual mood of levity and fun but strained in morbid awe to see the merchandise.

"Fifty dollars, and that's more'n he's worth!" one bidder declared.

But somebody disagreed with him and made it fifty-five. Presently the bid stood at sixty-three dollars and lagged a moment there. An Irishman, whose name historians have failed to record, spoke up at this juncture.

"By all the saints!" exclaimed he. "Are you going to do this thing? Actually auction it off? If you do, you will have ill luck for the remainder of your days!"

Deputy Sheriff Harrison, by no means at ease as an auctioneer should be, blanched a bit at the Irishman's warning and carelessly let his gavel fall. Sixty-three dollars, then, was the final offer, and the bidder stepped solemnly forward to claim his merchandise—the head of a very notorious man!

Sold on the auction block, right in the heart of the Southwest! Moreover, it was a forced sale because of attachment for debts against the man who had owned the head and who had made considerable sideshow money exhibiting it to the multitudes up and down the Pacific Coast. It was a handsome head, said the spectators; seeing it was well worth the dollar its owner charged. But after a time the public's lust for viewing it had been sated, and the owner had become mired in debt.

This was the head of a wild westerner who became the most feared bandit the American continent has ever known. Some historians go a step farther and say that his exploits in blood and plunder have not been excelled in all the history of the world. Yet, strangely, few persons today have more than a smattering of knowledge about him, even in his own beloved state of California, where he roamed.

His name was Joaquín Murrieta, and he is still the standard by which all other southwestern desperadoes are judged. No Jesse James, Grat Dalton, Pancho Villa, or Billy the Kid has ever equaled him and it is not at all surprising that honest people were curious to see the features of such a man, even in death. No one can say what ultimately became of the auctioned head. Likely it was a white elephant to the owner, who tired of it and finally threw it away. Conceivably it haunted him.

In spite of any revulsion against Murrieta's deeds, in spite of utter horror at the cruel, vengeful nature of his career, there exists a basic human sympathy for the man, at least in the story of the start of his criminal life. The worst bandit America has ever known was made so by the sordid, lustful natures of the very persons whom he later preyed upon. Given half a chance by fate, Murrieta might have been a noble character, a leader beloved by all. Consider his beginning:

Joaquín's first "crime" was that of being born a Mexican. At a moment in history when Anglo-Saxons were fired with gold fever as never before, Joaquín was a handsome young Latin living among them in California. He did a perfectly normal, legal thing in responding to the popular hysteria to go out and take gold ore and nuggets from the California hills. Luck went with him, for he made considerable money. Unfortunately he could not keep this fact a secret, and the "white" men became envious and angry.

Joaquín lived with his own countrymen. He had a beautiful young bride, Carmen. He had friends and relatives—indeed, California had been settled and developed by Mexican folk long before greedy "whites" came in—and he thought that happiness would be his forever. He could not understand why dirty American men contemptuously classed him and all Mexicans as "greasers." He had no inkling of the envy in their hearts.

To his utter amazement, therefore, one day while he, his brother, and his best friend were peacefully riding down the trail in open daylight, they were suddenly surrounded, captured, and tied hand and foot.

"Them's the very horses!" a fiery-eyed American exclaimed. "The greasers stole them!"

"String 'em up!"

"Ropes! Ropes! Hang th' dirty greasers!"

All manner of insults were hurled. A mob had formed, and before Joaquín could realize what was happening, his brother and his friend were dangling with necks broken. Only by the grace of God—and the fact that his horse was an old one known to be his own—did Joaquín escape their fate. The brother and friend had been riding stolen horses which they had purchased the day before in good faith, not knowing they were stolen. This fact could easily have been proven if the two men had been given but an hour's time.

Joaquín wept and trembled in fury at that injustice. Released from the mob, he went home in a miserable state. Only the prayers and gentle pleading of his beloved Carmen could soothe him. For days she worked to calm the spirit of her young husband. It was all terrible, she agreed, but there had been a crumb of justification for the American men; at least they thought they were dealing with horse thieves. A mistake is a mistake, however tragic. Let God in heaven be the one to fix the blame and administer the punishment. Gentle Carmen! She was a beloved bride.

"It is well," said Joaquín, at last. "I shall listen to your counsel, my Carmen. But I think only sorrow can live with us here. We will go away, back to Mexico, and live there forever in peace."

The young couple needed money for the trip and for establishing a new home, so Joaquín quietly went back to his gold claim for a final effort at mining. Success again attended him, so much, in fact, that the cupidity of "whites" was aroused again. They came openly to warn him.

"Get out!" they commanded. "No greasers'll be tolerated here!"

But Joaquín stood his ground. People of Spanish heritage had developed beautiful California long before the Americans had arrived. He was within his legal and moral rights. He thought the men were just blustery fellows, trying to bluff him. Instead, they attacked at once. With revolver butts and fists they knocked him prostrate, dazed him, and left him for dead. The news flew to Carmen, and while other Mexicans ran in abject fear she came bravely to her husband's rescue. Kneeling to help him, she was seen by the brutal men.

"That wench is likely looking!" one declared, grinning through his dirty beard. "I c'n use her, ha!"

Another had the same idea, and another, and still more.

24

Partly drunk, as usual, they fell to fighting among themselves for the pretty Mexican girl. Ignoring them at first, she
tried to go on with dressing Joaquín's wounds. She had
brought him back to his senses, but he was still helpless.

"I will take you home, away from these fighting men,"
she said to him. But even as the girl stooped to lift her husband, the others seized her, and before her husband's very
eyes they raped her. First one, then another, and another;
until the now fighting Carmen was so mistreated that she
was struck and killed.

Joaquín of course went virtually insane. Too weak from
his own wounds to move, he could only look on helplessly
at the most impossible of crimes. When eventually his
strength returned, the handsome young Mexican had become a brilliant madman, so keyed up by desperation and
anger that only one thing could ease him—the blood of revenge. He stayed so for the remainder of his days.

It is impossible in this space, and unnecessary as well, to
chronicle all the crimes of the bandit Murrieta. Not only
are they too many, but they also become increasingly repul-
sive; it is enough merely to record a few and hint at others.

A worker at Murphy's Mines in Calaveras County, in
April of 1850, was the first of Joaquín's victims. This miner
was walking quietly alone in the moonlight, when a finely
dressed man stepped from a night shadow and lifted a dagger.

"Have pity!" the miner begged. "What have I done to
you? You need not have stabbed me to take my purse!"

"You are one of the twenty who beat me and killed my
wife!" The accusation came, like the death sentence it was,
from the mouth of a snarling fiend.

Trembling with the passion of his anger, Murrieta stood
over his victim and stabbed him many times until Murrieta's
hands were bloody and tears of emotion flowed. (He told of
this himself, later.) Over the bloody corpse he stood, lifted

25

his eyes to heaven, and cried, "I swear not to rest until I have slain the last one! Thou, Carmen, whose sweet spirit watches over me, shall be avenged. Before I die the blood of all our enemies shall flow!" It was a terrible vow—so terrible that today the reading of it sounds like some fantastic melodrama.

In the succeeding months Joaquín Murrieta became the mystery outlaw of California. A man of high talents, aristocratic and well educated, he easily collected a band of followers, most of whom were as adventurous and hardy as himself. In the course of the years a legend has formed about him and his band which makes him appear to be a sort of Robin Hood who pillaged only the rich in order to help the poor. But the legend has little foundation. The men who joined him were experts at robbing and killing. They deserve no admiration. Their only god was the god of cruelty.

Eight harmless Chinese, working unobtrusively along an isolated riverbank, were encountered one day by the Murrieta gang. Joaquín's lieutenant was a particularly bestial man named Three-finger Jack García, who had lost two fingers in the Mexican war and whose sole pleasure in life was to take other men's lives. He saw the Chinese, tied their queues together, and alone dragged them trembling into the bandit camp.

"What will you do with them, Jack?" Joaquín asked. "They have no money for us to take."

"But our brave men are tired from riding and need amusement," the brutal lieutenant answered. Then, for sheer pleasure and show, he personally stabbed all eight of them to death in the light of the campfire. Murrieta upbraided him for such wanton cruelty, concluding with the accusation that "your soul, Jack, is as black as Satan himself!"

But hardly a week had passed before the bandits encountered four American men. Murrieta ordered them robbed, but with as little bloodshed as possible, because he did not want to have to flee from the territory just then. The bandits approached the Americans cautiously.

"Wait!" whispered Joaquín, when he was close enough to identify the men. "Send Jack to me."

When Three-finger Jack came before his chieftain, he heard his orders in glee.

"Not only will I allow you to kill them," Murrieta growled in unholy anger, "but this time I order you to slay them and with their bodies do what you will. Three of those men were among those who attacked me, then killed my wife. The fourth deserves his fate for being in such company!"

Jack García sprang to his task like a fiend from hell. With his companions he fired a volley of shots at the Americans which knocked three from their horses and badly wounded them.

"Ah, you recognize me now? I am Joaquín!" the bandit shouted to the four victims and stood by while Jack got in his bloody pleasure. Parts of human bodies were scattered all over the roadway when Jack was done.

Joaquín commended him for his thoroughness and added, "Whenever I find any of those men who ruined my life, who killed my brother and my Carmen and tortured me that day, your knife shall not rust from lack of use, my friend García!"

Because he championed their cause, nearly all the Mexicans in the territory were at least partly sympathetic and friendly toward Murrieta, and among them he had an abundance of willing spies. Moreover, these people spread the news of his exploits and thereby helped to terrorize the countryside whenever he was known to be near. Men who had been in the party that attacked him and his wife began to fear death at any moment. They hardly dared to leave their homes, and never at night would they go outdoors. One night about midnight three of them disguised themselves and tried to slip out of the country to safety. The next day their bodies were found pinned to the earth with great stakes, their eyes gouged out, and their tongues gone. Three-finger Jack had been given discretionary powers again.

At times Murrieta's band totaled more than two hundred men, and usually they operated in two or three separate units, meeting occasionally at a central headquarters situated in a well-concealed and easily defended valley. Each of the units devoted itself to pillage and plunder, rapine and death. They stole literally thousands of horses and periodically drove their stolen herds into Mexico for sale. They robbed stores and mines and other places where there was an abundance of booty; or if big loot was not available they would slay and disembowel a lone man for the few dollars and the pistols he carried. If there were no victims to rob, the bands amused themselves by finding some to kill.

Joaquín often left his *compadres* and went boldly into the villages to operate alone. Monte was the fashionable game of the day, and he frequently dropped into a gambling hall for diversion. In all his robberies he never appeared twice in the same costume, and he often resorted to false mustaches and beards and new clothing for disguise.

On one occasion a distinguished-looking young Mexican —apparently the son of a wealthy rancher—had been visiting a mining town for several days. His friendliness was marked, and his popularity with the girls was obvious. He had a smile of greeting for everyone. He listened carefully whenever the people talked of Joaquín Murrieta's latest deeds and expressed sorrow when the charred bodies of two men were found in the remains of a fire near the town. The handiwork of Murrieta was seen. The bold bandit's escapades were a constant source of conversation and worry. One day in a village saloon, some swaggering fellow waxed eloquent.

"I wish to God I could get just one glimpse of this here Murrieta!" the man roared. "The trouble is, everybody is afraid of him. I wish I could have just one chance. I'd snatch out my gun and shoot him down like the snake he is!"

The handsome young Mexican man rose from his card table and leaped, panther-like, to a chair. There he stood, poised in consummate grace and menace.

"You have your chance, señor!" said he, calmly. "I am Joaquín Murrieta!"

Joaquín waited a moment while the audience stared. Then he jumped through the door, mounted his horse, and dashed away amid a hail of bullets. The boaster had made no move to shoot him when Joaquín declared himself in the saloon.

Another instance of Joaquín's sheer audacity occurred when one sheriff in the territory grew desperate. This particular sheriff had made a few sallies with his deputies and had been lucky enough to escape with his life. He didn't know which way to turn next; if he searched in the northern part of his jurisdiction, Joaquín would strike in the south; if he hastened to the south, Joaquín would attack in the north. So the officer posted a large sign on a tree on the main street of his town:

REWARD

For the capture of

Joaquín Murrieta

dead or alive,

I will pay $500.

The sheriff signed and witnessed the poster and repeated his promise verbally here and there in the area.

Within a few hours a horseman rode down the main street and stopped in front of the sign. All at once he laughed out loud. Then, while a few curious persons stared from the sidewalks, he leaned down, wrote something on the bottom of the sign, and rode on. When the curious onlookers walked over they read this postscript:

And I will pay $10,000
Joaquín Murrieta

Though he was only a short distance away, the hastily formed posse failed to catch him.

There were caves and many Mexican dwellings in the hills, and there were secret tunnels leading from homes to caves and from one home to another. Strange signals were used to inform the bandit leader, as well. It was said later that at night sundry lights telegraphed information about the countryside, and that by day the hanging of washed clothes on a line in a particular way would carry warnings. Two sheets on a line beside a Mexican shack high on a hillside could be seen for many miles. Two more sheets and then two more could string out the warning through a canyon, across a valley, and into mountains beyond—hours ahead of any sheriff or posse—and who could prove that sheets on a line were anything but innocent tokens of washday?

"Ah, ha!" the reader may exclaim. "This is fiction, the romantic imaginations of a scenario writer, for I myself have seen the signals on the movie screen and the episode of the posted reward!" True. Scenario writers are clever. They recognize drama when and where they find it and lift it from history to fit their own needs. At least three "gay bandit" stories have been screened in which the life of Joaquín Murrieta was drawn upon for material, and none of them was historically accurate save in a few details. All of them inserted a love story with much guitar-playing, serenading of lovely señoritas, and silhouetting of profiles against the Southwestern sunset. Joaquín might have fitted this picture very well, for he was in truth a handsome *caballero;* but the modern motion picture invariably stops there and never shows the unutterable cruelties of the man.

Joaquín's second love was a notable one. When he had killed most of the men who ravaged his Carmen and had gained great wealth by robbery, Joaquín returned to Mexico and encountered there a girl he had known earlier.

Clarita is recorded as having been even lovelier than Carmen. Carmen had leaned toward plumpness; Clarita was slender, stately, and delicately beautiful. She stayed with Joaquín through many months of his hardest campaigning in crime. She became a sort of goddess in the camp of the daring bandit whose love she had won. She rode with him on many of his robberies and looked on passively when he or his lieutenants killed or tortured their victims.

Another young criminal in Joaquín's band took a fancy to Clarita soon after she joined the desperadoes. Joaquín soon learned of the other man's attentions.

"You like Clarita, eh?" Joaquín accosted him one day. "Well, well, that is fine! You shall be alone with her for a while, my loyal one!"

Smart enough to know he faced death, the man pleaded for mercy.

"But Señor!" Joaquín protested, "I did not say I would kill you! I shall do nothing like that. Clarita herself shall do all the choosing."

The rival lover was then hung by his heels with a frayed rope from a limb that protruded over a sheer cliff. While the stiff breeze of the high mountaintop swung him to and fro, Clarita was placed under the tree about fifteen feet away with a bushel or so of egg-sized rocks and told to have her fun. Nor did she dare disobey! She knew only too well the nature of her lover. For hours the bandits laughed listening to the rocks striking the bottom of the deep canyon under the swinging man, until the swaying and the sharp rocks finally severed the rope and concluded the entertainment.

Nobody ever knew exactly how many men fell victims to Murrieta and his gang, but they numbered in the hundreds. And the gold and money they stole, plus the horses and incidental plunder, must have totaled millions. On several occasions the band got more than $50,000 in a single raid. Usually these major robberies were inflicted on stores of gold that mining communities had collected.

Always the fortress of good luck seemed to protect Murrieta. Of his men he lost many; sometimes as many as a

dozen of his followers would be slain in combat with deputies and citizens' police or would be captured and hanged.
But the leader himself, foremost always in the fighting,
would escape. He did suffer a few wounds, but he would
hide out until he recovered and then renew his bloody sallies.
After each loss of comrades his comeback seemed to have
added fury. If ever he knew just which Americans had done
the actual killing, these he would track down first and slay
with special cruelty in a mad lust for revenge.

Repeatedly the authorities determined to put a stop to
Murrieta and his dreadful deeds, but this was no ordinary
bad man they had to deal with. A quick-trigger gunman
could always be taken one way or another, usually by a law-
man who was a shade faster on the draw and equally cool-
headed. An ordinary horse thief, killer, or stage robber could
usually be hunted down by a posse and strung from a limb.
But not Joaquín Murrieta. Joaquín was a veritable phantom
—a phantom backed by a small army of his own and aided
by many spies and by the abject fear which his exploits had
instilled in the people. This fear, moreover, was entirely
justified, for it was truly said that Murrieta would do anything.

A Texan named Harry Love, who had fought in the
Mexican-American war, was the officer who finally got
Murrieta.

In May, 1853, the legislature and the Governor of California authorized Love, a captain, to organize a band of state
police for the express purpose of running down Joaquín
Murrieta. No money was provided to pay the police, and
each volunteer had to furnish his horse, arms, and provisions.
Yet Love had his men well trained and organized in a very
short time. He chose twenty whose ability and valor he
trusted and started grimly on the trail of the bandit king.
Friends watched them depart with much apprehension, be-

33

cause such groups had met only torture and death heretofore.

But Captain Love was a determined man and a skillful one. After careful scouting, his men began to close in on their enemy. One day near the village of Tulare they spied a column of smoke in the distance.

"It may not be important," said Captain Love, "but we will do well to take no chances. Let us investigate."

In a little while they unexpectedly came on Murrieta and six of his friends around a fire. For once—and for the last time—in his career the usually wary bandit was surprised. He, Three-finger Jack, and the others jumped to their horses, fleeing in a rain of lead. Love's officers dashed after them at full speed.

The police needed the luck that rode with them then. Murrieta's horses were more accustomed to hard runs and were moving away from their pursuers. Captain Love chased Murrieta and by good fortune wounded the bandit. Even as he lay dying, Murrieta fired his two remaining pistol shots at his adversaries. Then he realized that the end had come.

"It is enough," he called to Captain Love. "Shoot no more, please. I have finished my plan. It is well that I die now. I have had my revenge."

Three-finger Jack fled on foot, badly wounded, for more than a mile before a bullet finally killed him. Of all the bandits attacked, only one escaped.

It was Captain Love, ordinarily a very mild-mannered man not given to show, who cut off the head of Murrieta, not to exhibit it at a dollar a ticket—that idea occurred to him later, when so much popular interest was manifested—but to collect the rewards that had been offered. These rewards totaled thousands of dollars, and Love needed the money to pay his valorous men and himself as well. But nobody would pay a reward without absolute proof that

Murrieta was dead. Sworn testimony was not sufficient. But there was one way, said the captain, who then obtained a sharp knife and a bottle of alcohol.

When its official purpose had been served, the bandit's head "went on the stage." Garish posters were stuck up about each community where it was shown. An example:

JOAQUÍN'S HEAD
Is to be seen at King's Corner
Halleck and Sansome Streets,
Admission One Dollar.

So the notice read in one town. The morbid people, happy to know that the head was at last severed from its body, thronged in. After a while, however, the crowds stopped coming, and the showman went into debt. That's why Deputy Sheriff Harrison auctioned off the head.

The Irishman who prophesied ill luck to the auctioneer spoke truly. Not long after that day's bidding, Deputy Harrison was placing his pistol on a desk, when it accidentally discharged and killed him.

3

BLUFF AND BLOOD AT TOMBSTONE

THERE NEVER was any particular reason why the Clantons should have hated the Earps with such unforgiving fury. It just so happened that the town of Tombstone collected two incompatible strata of human society; the Clantons had bluster enough to lead one of them, and the Earps had guts enough to lead the other. In the final showdown, most of their respective followers stood back and let them take care of the bloody business alone.

It was inevitable that the two factions should eventually clash. They endured a lot from each other. Hatred sizzled and smoldered for years, then was climaxed in fifteen seconds when four of the Earp gang met four of the Clanton gang in a sidewalk gun battle. Reverberations of that social thunder are still heard in the old Southwest—indeed, stories of sensational events at Tombstone will be heard as long as men find leisure to talk under the southwestern sun. No town's history is more colorful or is fraught with more rip-roaring drama. Historians often disagree about details, but never about the major episodes. Foremost among the latter in sheer gripping interest is the unpleasantness between the Earps and the Clantons.

Time has made Wyatt Earp and his henchmen the heroes of the struggle and has given the Clantons a record possibly blacker than they deserved. Neither side was steeped in saintliness, but it happens that the Earps did have the authority of a nominal law behind them, and the Clantons did not. That makes a big difference now.

It was a masterful piece of law enforcement by Wyatt Earp, in fact, which really started the feud. Wyatt had come to the booming Tombstone—a very lively town despite its name—from gun-totin' Dodge City, Kansas, and had stepped right into a job as United States deputy marshal.

He was eminently fitted for the job. The Clantons found that out when a contemptible little gambler named Johnny O'Rourke murdered a friend of the Clantons. Somebody put Johnny on a horse and dashed madly with him to the custody of Marshal Earp, interrupting Wyatt in a card game at the Oriental Gambling Emporium. Leisurely, Mr. Earp locked the murderer inside a bowling alley. Then he picked up his shotgun, walked to the middle of the street, lit a cigar, and waited.

He didn't wait long. Down Tough Nut Street, which was Tombstone's main thoroughfare in 1880, came a subdued roar, perhaps the most ominous noise known—the bustle and rumble of grim-faced citizens determined to hang a fellow man. Its volume was increasing rapidly. Like an all-consuming mass of lava flowed this mob of five-hundred-odd men. As they approached the block, Wyatt Earp spat out his cigar and cocked his gun. "Recommend you boys don't come no farther," he spoke a little loudly, so all could hear. The mobsters presented a solid front from sidewalk to sidewalk, every man armed, most of them with guns now unholstered.

"Ain't no sense in all this, gentlemen," Wyatt continued, still very calm. "Seems like you all oughtn't to make no fool play like this."

They halted now and stared at the lone man—a rather tall,

37

mustached individual holding a shotgun, thus greeting five-hundred citizens of his town.

"Whar hev you hid that murderin' sneak?" Ike Clanton snarled. "We aim to string him up!"

"He's in the bowling alley," Wyatt answered promptly. "But he is in my custody. I am an officer of the law. You won't get him."

"The hell we won't!" The rumble of the mob swelled again in an awesome crescendo.

"You heard me!" Wyatt's eyes took on that dark squint, which many a man had behld as his last sight on earth. Most of the men in the front line of the mob knew that squint and respected it. Wyatt continued speaking.

"You heard me! I said he was my prisoner, and he is. If he murdered anybody, he'll hang by law. You know that. But not now. . . . I know—I ain't blind—I know you can all shoot. I see yore guns. But as shore as the devil made side-winders I'll git one of you, maybe more! Quiet now. I aim to kill the first man that moves. I got two barrels, and I ain't skittish none!"

You could have heard the marshal's watch ticking for the next few seconds. And Arizona history reveals that Johnny O'Rourke lived to see another day—several more days, in fact. Johnny was escorted to jail that same afternoon and later managed to escape—escaping so fast and so far that Arizona did not again see hide nor hair of him. He had committed murder, right enough, and it was a levelheaded citizen who had hastily put him behind his own saddle and galloped him to Marshal Earp's custody.

Possibly if Johnny hadn't escaped, the Clantons would have cooled off and realized that Marshal Earp had simply carried out his sworn duty. But Johnny had gone, and he stayed gone. There were people who said that Earp helped him escape, and probably all the Clantons died believing it.

The feeling doubtless added to the Clantons' resentment against Wyatt, a resentment born with Wyatt's masterful bluff. The Clantons, you see, were pretty proud of their own reputations as fighters and gunmen; yet here a new, quiet-mannered officer from Kansas had stolen their thunder. The bluff set everybody to talking.

Then on top of this episode came another little drama at Tombstone, partly accidental, which added fuel to an already glowing fire of enmity. Sheer chance or circumstance seemed to control this event, which again, involved Wyatt Earp, and a two-fisted trigger artist named Curly Bill, a close friend of the Clantons and one of their partners in crime.

Curly Bill posed as a cowboy, which he was in part. He had cows all right, but his manner of getting them was the basis of his ill repute. He just took them, without due process of law.

One night he was carousing with some cowboy friends in Tombstone's gay dance halls. For once they were reasonably quiet, carrying on just a normal amount of friendly drinking, gambling, dancing, and such. At midnight they decided to ride back home. Outside and mounted, they took one last fling at pleasure: they jerked out their pistols and fired a few .45 volleys at the man in the moon. Just noisy boys, you understand.

But Tombstone had recently put a ban on unnecessary shooting and made it punishable by a fine and a few days in jail. When the pistols went off, City Marshal Frederick White must have jumped clear out of bed. Soon he stuck his head out his door near by.

"What in hell's going on out here?" he roared.

The cowboys laughed and scattered. Presently Marshal White, now dressed, stalked out, cussin'.

"These hell-raisin' cowpunchers hev got to be stopped!"

he grumbled. He saw one of them in the moon shadow of a building, went over, and stuck a pistol in his face. The cowboy was Curly Bill.

"Gimme yore gun, Bill," Marshal White demanded. "You cain't shoot up this town no more like that!"

Now Curly Bill had long held to a pet theory that a six-shooter is best kept loaded against real need, so he actually hadn't done any of that night's shooting at all. He resented this insult from the marshal. He protested, but at length he lifted his gun and held it to Mr. White, butt first.

At that instant somebody suddenly grabbed Curly from behind. In a flash a struggle ensued. Curly's gun roared, Marshal White fell dead, and the newcomer's own pistol crashed down on Curly's head. The newcomer was Wyatt Earp.

Wyatt had thought Curly was resisting the city officer. Curly was knocked out and dragged to jail bleeding. While he recovered there, nursing his scalp wound, he also nursed a hatred of Wyatt Earp, of all Wyatt's several brothers, and of everybody who maintained friendship for Wyatt Earp, now and hereafter.

He fostered this hatred even when Wyatt testified that the shooting was accidental and so helped clear Curly, fostered it, snarling, on the morning he finally got on his horse and rode out of town, free. Curly Bill, about the most dangerous cattle rustler and robber in the Southwest, was now a sworn enemy of all the Earps. And Curly Bill was hand-in-hand in deviltry with the Clantons.

We moderns would have called the Clantons gangsters. Rumrunning, dope-peddling and kidnaping weren't fashionable crimes then, and the Clantons lived in the criminal order of the day: they stole cows, robbed stagecoaches, and committed murder. The isolation of Tombstone and the absence at first even of railroads forced them to stay in or near the same community and dodge the same police (unlike our modern gangsters who can cavort all over a nation). Hence it is easy to see how enmity between outlaws and officers could grow and become personal. Neighborliness thereby played a strange role.

Strangely, too, the Clanton gang of desperadoes had much political and military power. They maintained a front of respectability. They were hand in hand with the sheriff of Cochise County, John Behan. (Tombstone was the county seat.) By political maneuvering or by intimidation they often controlled whole precincts at elections and halted many rather superficial processes of law. They walked the streets of Tombstone unmolested, perhaps to flee before a posse before nightfall. They spread terror and death about the countryside, shooting and killing from ambush—only to show up in town the next day meek and humble as lambs. Tombstone, in the eighteen eighties, was too busy mining silver and getting rich to bother much about law enforcement. There wasn't much law to enforce, anyway; generally it was a quick-on-the-draw proposition.

Ike Clanton and his brothers Billy and Phineas (called Finn) headed the gang, and "Old Man" Clanton, the father, was a hellion in his own right. Their henchmen were Curly Bill, two tough and terrible individuals named Tom and Frank McLowery, a dastardly road agent and murderer named Frank Stillwell, and such assorted thugs and thieves as Johnnie Ringo, Pete Spence, and their ilk. This chronicle could fill volumes with their blood-curdling exploits and then tell only half the story. Each exploit usually ran them smack against the law, and the law in Tombstone usually meant either Wyatt or Virgil Earp or their friends.

It is essential at this point to introduce a secondary but nevertheless highly important figure in the blood feud between the Earps and the Clantons. He is rather like the strong

42

minor character in a good stage play who threatens to out-
shine the hero because of his fine acting. And Doc Holliday
was a fine actor! History in the sun country still teems with
the memory of him. He was short-lived, but he was potent.
As a lad back in the old South he had killed some Negro
boys who pre-empted his swimming hole. As an adventurous dentist in Texas he shot down a man who tried to
take away his dance-hall sweetie. He and Wyatt Earp met
in the Texas Panhandle and cottoned to each other right
away. Soon he turned up in Tombstone as a close friend of
the Earp brothers.

One day Miss Nellie Cashman, proprietress of the Russ
House Restaurant in Tombstone, served beans for dinner.
(In Miss Nellie's place the customers sat around one long
table, family style.) Perhaps they were not her very best
beans, although Miss Nellie cooked as an artist paints, for
love of creative endeavor. And being along in years, she
mothered most of the men of the community. The men in
turn regarded her with profound admiration and respect.
They enjoyed eating there. Doc Holliday especially liked
her hospitality.

One of the McLowery boys drifted into town and went
to Miss Nellie's for lunch on this particular day. Doc was
eating there, too, but the outlaw didn't see him at first. Mc-
Lowery was in a nasty mood.

"Hey, woman, ain'tcha got nothing but beans?" he
growled at Miss Nellie. "Good God, rustle some fittin' grub
out here!"

Miss Nellie's mouth dropped in awe and anger. But she
did not have to fight her own battle, for once.

"Reckon them is dee-licious beans, mister!" a laconic,
ominously cool voice spoke.

The speaker had risen from his seat. He was tall, extremely thin, and well-groomed. He stood a little stooped now,

with his right hand on the handle of his gun like a steel trap set to spring.

"Reckon you jest craves more and more of them," he continued. "That whole dish, there, is to be et. Miss Nellie, she'd take that as a compliment to her fine cooking. We all hereabouts believe Miss Nellie assays tolerable high as a cook, Mister McLowery."

Mister McLowery had good nerves. He had done his share of killing, and he was noted from Denver to Hermosillo as a dangerous gunman. But his reputation was almost juvenile compared to Doc Holliday's.

He stared a moment or two at Doc's hard eyes, noted Doc's poise, and quietly ate the entire dish of beans. Then as quietly he rose and left the dining room.

Not a shot was fired, but the looks were murderous. Old-timers will tell you today that the incident added much to the Clantons' hatred of the Earps. McLowery, a Clanton gangster; Holliday, an intimate of Wyatt Earp. Pride was a fierce thing in the old Southwest.

Doc Holliday was not particularly malicious or mean, but he was a flash-tempered killer unafraid of death. He was a "lunger" who wagered openly that tuberculosis would kill him before a bullet did. He dressed like a dandy, concealing his hollow form admirably in his social life, but to those whom he despised he suggested a deadly ghost. He had only a few intimate friends, and of these he loved Wyatt Earp most. Their brotherly affection is a still-growing legend in the Southwest, even as their great feud with the Clantons has become a western Iliad of sensation and tragedy.

Ike Clanton had some brothers, but Wyatt Earp had more. Besides Virgil Earp, there were Morgan, James, and Warren, five in all—five big, blond fellows who had been lured westward in 1879 by the startling news of the silver discovery at Tombstone. Ed Schieffelin had made the discovery and named the town when he found some rich nuggets between the outstretched hands of two skeletons. But Schieffelin didn't live to enjoy the subsequent turbulence. He and Wyatt Earp might have been good friends, too.

Wyatt first worked in Tombstone as a shotgun messenger on the stagecoach for the Wells Fargo Express Company and held that job even while he served as United States Deputy Marshal for the district. He never fired a shot during the six months he held the Wells Fargo job, but the stagecoach was never robbed, either. Six months without a holdup was big news and testified better than anything else to Wyatt's prestige in the community. Later Morgan Earp also served as shotgun messenger for Wells Fargo, and in time all the Earp brothers were either elected officers or deputized enforcers of Tombstone's law.

Their progression in popular esteem at Tombstone rankled constantly in the Clantons' minds, particularly in Ike Clanton's. Ike made innumerable boasts about what he was going to do to the Earps some day. He never quite got around to it when he was sober, but occasionally he got drunk, and on one spree he actually took gun in hand and set forth to kill his enemy Wyatt.

The records do not show exactly what happened, but Wyatt lived for many years after the episode. "Someone" had mischievously tied Ike's hands behind him and sent him reeling back down the street. Nobody laughed as uproariously as Doc Holliday, and the Earp boys all wore broad grins.

The murder of Bud Philpot, a stage driver, was probably the episode which brought the Earps and the Clantons to their grand showdown. Bud drove the stagecoach to Benson. Bob Paul sat with him as shotgun messenger, theoretically guarding against the ever-present road agents. But Paul was evidently inattentive that day, and when the stage rounded a curve a few miles out of the village of Contention, three masked horsemen suddenly appeared.

"Put up yore hands!"

The command was not a gentle one, but it was not obeyed. Paul's hands went up, but his shotgun was in them. He blasted down a load of buckshot at the nearest man.

Instantly, of course, the robbers answered. An unseen man on the other side of the road put a bullet through Bud Philpot's heart, and Bud toppled from the high seat down between the horses' hoofs. The gunfire frightened the two teams, who suddenly bolted, got a head start on the robbers, and jerked the stagecoach wildly down the rocky road.

Passengers inside screamed. One Tombstone citizen, who sat on the outside rear seat, was shot in the back and killed, but Paul eventually got control of the horses and drove the stage safely into Benson, with the $80,000 it carried intact. A searching party picked up the two bodies and carried them to Tombstone, and Sheriff Behan headed out with a posse forthwith.

Wyatt, Morgan, and Virgil Earp were in the posse. Behan had included them, not because he wanted to, but because their reputations as officers were greater than his own and no posse could truly represent Tombstone without them. Moreover, they were dead shots, skilled at trailing and unafraid of the devil himself. Behan was a Clanton sympathizer, but he respected the Earps.

This group of officers soon learned that Jim Crane, Harry Head, and Bill Leonard, all allied with the Clanton gang, had stopped the stage and done the killings, but rumor held that a fourth, and as yet unknown, man had been with them, too. For seventeen days the officers trailed the outlaws and returned eventually without results. Crane, Head, and Leonard had escaped across the New Mexico line.

Back at home the Earps learned to their astonishment that their own pal, Doc Holliday, now stood accused of having been the fourth man, the bandit across the road who had shot Bud Philpot in the heart. The Tombstone *Epitaph,* a fearless newspaper normally friendly to the Earps, was even intimating as much.

Nobody can prove to this day that Doc wasn't guilty, nor has anybody ever proved that he was. Doc himself received news of his accusation with biting sarcasm and a series of pretty good alibis. The situation smoldered for several weeks. Sheriff Johnny Behan did nothing about it, for the simple reason that Johnny, together with everyone else in Cochise County, had a profound respect for Doc Holliday's uncanny skill with a gun. Doc said, in effect, "What if I am guilty? What are you going to do about it?" But Wyatt Earp swore that Doc was innocent.

The Clanton boys jumped on the scandal as choice meat. They talked about it, kept it alive and hot. This was their first chance to spike the consistently good reputation of the Earps' henchman, and they made the most of it. But it caused Doc Holliday to mark them for death.

People were clamoring for capture and punishment of the three known stage robbers, and in a piece of private detective work, Wyatt Earp made a rather bold move. He hunted up Ike Clanton in Tombstone one day and asked for a private conference with him. It was strange that these two blood enemies should thus get together and make a deal, but they did. Both later testified to it.

Ike agreed to set a trap for the three stage robbers, who were members of his gang, so the Earps could capture them. In return the Clantons were to receive the total reward offered, $3,600. Besides Wyatt and Ike, only one man, a telegraph operator, knew anything of the deal. But before the plan was consummated, the operator got drunk and talked.

47

Ike Clanton accused Wyatt of revealing the secret. Wyatt vehemently denied it, but Clanton just called him a liar.

From that point the climax approached rapidly. The Clantons came to town, swearing vengeance on the Earps for the manner in which Wyatt had "tricked" them. And Doc Holliday wanted to even the score for his friend Wyatt. When the Clantons arrived that morning, the news quickly spread that they had come to town to have it out and would kill the Earps on sight. Doc Holliday heard the news, smiled that sardonic, deadly grin of his, walked over to the Oriental Gambling House, and strapped a sawed-off shotgun to his shoulder.

Shortly after noon, Wyatt, Morgan, and Virgil Earp and Doc Holliday, all armed, met on the street.

"Let's go settle it, boys," Wyatt said. The four started off at a walk, heading for the O. K. Corral.

Sheriff Behan saw them a block before they reached the corral and ran to stop them. Standing in front of them on the sidewalk, he held up a restraining hand.

"Halt!" he commanded. "As sheriff of this county I must stop this! Go back. I will do what I can to disarm the Clantons. You men must not fight!"

His official orders made no ruffle in the grim progress of the Earp band. They missed not a step—just elbowed him to one side and marched on, four abreast. Wise citizens on the street had already done their duty by themselves and disappeared from sight.

Sheriff Behan followed the Earps, protesting, until he reached the door of Fly's Photograph Gallery. There, he too allowed the law of self-preservation to triumph over the law of the land. He stepped into Fly's and squatted behind a window sill, where he could peek out.

Ike Clanton, Billy Clanton (a boy), and Tom and Frank

McLowery were standing with their backs to the corral wall, their pistols still holstered.

The Earps drew first, as they walked, but they gave fair warning—if, indeed, any had been needed.

"You fellows have been swearing to kill us," Wyatt said, "now's yore chance to make good. Draw!"

No two people have ever told exactly the same story of what happened then. But the details don't matter a great deal. For fifteen seconds the O. K. Corral sounded like a battlefield. Thirty or more shots were fired, and gun smoke became so dense that aim was poor on some of them.

Morgan Earp shot Billy Clanton, because the boy was quickest to level his gun. The lad fell dying but raised himself on his elbows and kept on shooting for several seconds.

Tom McLowery jumped toward his brother's horse, either to mount it and flee or to get a shotgun from the saddle holster. It was later maintained that Tom was unarmed, but if he was the Earps certainly had no way of knowing it, and in any event he shouldn't have been.

When Tom started for the horse, the cool and unexcitable Doc Holliday swung his sawed-off shotgun from its shoulder sling and pulled both triggers. The hole in Tom's body was big enough to put a gallon bucket in, the undertaker said later.

Tom's brother saw Doc Holliday's maneuver and drew a bead on Doc.

"Here's where I get even with you!" Frank shouted. But he had already been badly wounded by Wyatt Earp and should never have paused to speak.

Doc Holliday ran toward him, shooting his pistol as he ran. Then in the instant that Frank fired Doc turned his extremely thin body sideways, making a very narrow target indeed. Frank's bullet barely creased him.

Frank, who was suffering badly, then turned to kill Morgan Earp. Wyatt shouted a warning to his brother. In a flash Morgan and Doc Holliday both blazed away at McLowery, and the man fell with a bullet through his brain. Nobody knows whether Morgan or Doc did the actual killing.

Meanwhile, young Billy Clanton, prone on the curbing, was praying loudly for "just one more shot, God, just one more shot!" and struggling to gather his strength for it.

Tremblingly he lifted his head, then his pistol. He tried to aim, while Doc Holliday and the three deadly Earps looked on motionless, hesitant to shoot any man, even a Clanton, when he was down.

But the boy couldn't quite make it. His pistol slipped out of his hand unfired. The bullet that killed him had passed through a pocket containing an endearing letter from his sweetheart. And his last whispered request was that his boots be removed before he died. The request was granted.

But where had tough-and-terrible Ike Clanton been during all the furious fighting? Where was Ike, the gang leader who had sworn to kill the Earps on sight and who had come to town that day especially to get revenge on Wyatt?

Ike was no fool, no matter what else he could be called. People who knew the Earps and the deadly Doc Holliday say that Ike Clanton showed more judgment than any of his crowd. When the fireworks started, Ike did what the rabbit does: he "histed" his white tail and ran. It was days before anybody saw him again.

When the atmosphere had cleared a little, pompous Sheriff Behan reappeared on the scene.

"I will have to arrest you, Wyatt," he told that individual.

Wyatt Earp looked at his old-time personal and political enemy. And Wyatt's eyes, as has been said before, could be as menacing as his guns. The snort of contempt Wyatt Earp gave Sheriff Behan in that moment must have been notable.

"Next week, maybe, if I'm a mind for it," calmly said

Mr. Earp. And Mr. Behan very prudently did nothing.

For weeks thereafter the excitement continued. The Earps did eventually stand trial, but Judge Spicer ruled that they had acted as officers of the law, and they were freed. Their technical freedom by no means satisfied everybody. For all their justice and fairness, the Earps had plenty of enemies still alive. There were a few abortive attempts at lynching, but the old feud soon settled down to a slower process of retribution and revenge.

Months later Wyatt, Virgil, and Doc Holliday were talking late one night in the Oriental Gambling Emporium. Play hadn't been very lively, and conversation was favored. After a while, Virgil rose and walked out the front door, heading for home and bed. Immediately a fusillade of guns was heard, and Wyatt and Doc rushed out to find Virgil apparently dying. Nobody knew who shot him. He lingered for weeks and finally recovered after a fashion, but one arm was useless thereafter, and a body injury pained him for years. As soon as possible, however, he joined his brother in quiet detective work. They were interrupted by another tragedy.

Morgan Earp was playing pool one night with his friend Bob Hatch at the rear of Hatch's saloon. Near Morgan was a back door with a glass pane in it. Without warning, out of the darkness a shot crashed through the glass, struck Morgan in the back, passed on through him, and hit George Berry in the thigh at the front of the saloon.

Morgan's brothers were hastily summoned. They gathered around him, and when Wyatt bent down, Morgan whispered something. Wyatt nodded his head.

"The game's over," Morgan spoke a moment later, loudly enough for all to hear. Then he died.

The assassins were definitely out to wreak revenge on the clan of Earp. Whispered warnings came to them from everywhere. At Christmas Doc Holliday received a "gift" neatly tied up in ribbon and cotton, but when he opened the dainty box a .45-caliber bullet fell out. It contained no card, but Doc needed none.

Nobody knew who had made the cowardly attack on Virgil, or who had shot Morgan to death through the saloon door that night. Either Ike Clanton or his rather nondescript brother Finn, both of whom did most of their fighting verbally, might well have been guilty, but they managed to have fairly good alibis at both times. Wyatt Earp was not fooled, however. He knew Tombstone; and he knew his enemies. So did Doc Holliday. On top of this, the dying Morgan must have told something important when he whispered that last message to his brother.

After Morgan's death, Ike Clanton and Frank Stillwell, who had become Ike's closest henchman, had discreetly gone to Tucson. Wyatt and Doc knew this and announced that they would accompany Morgan's remains back to Kansas and would pass through Tucson that night.

They were shrewd enough to know that Ike and Stillwell would fall right into the trap if the news reached them, which it did. But at the last minute the wily Mr. Ike Clanton dodged again. He stayed away from the railroad station on a pretense of watching for his two enemies at a hotel. Stillwell agreed to hide behind some freight cars near the spot where the incoming engine must stop. His idea was to shoot Doc or Wyatt or both through the coach window as their train pulled out.

But Doc and Wyatt, keenly alert, got off the train and cautiously began walking around the yard, ostensibly stretching from the weariness of travel. The yard was poorly lighted. They walked about for several minutes while the trainmen were busy at their affairs.

Bang—bang—bang!

Quick shots sounded up near the front of the train.

"Cowboys celebratin', I reckon," said the engineer casually to his fireman.

Doc and Wyatt boarded the rear of the train as it was moving, a hundred yards or so down the track. Calmly they went in and resumed their old seats.

"Warm this evenin', ain't it gentlemen?" Wyatt remarked conversationally to their neighbor passengers, and the train talk continued in friendly manner for some time, until they all stretched out to rest a bit and snore. At daybreak the railyard watchman found a man dead from bullet wounds near the end of a string of freight cars. Later the body was identified as that of Frank Stillwell.

Wyatt and Doc did not wash their hands of this affair as easily as they had hoped. For once they were outside the law, and most of the citizenry thereabouts knew it. Much of their former prestige suffered, and when, therefore, Sheriff Behan exhibited warrants for their arrest some days later, these two stalwart sons of violence decided that the time had come to move.

But they did not kowtow to Johnny Behan! They bawled out that worthy with a prime assortment of cusswords and told him to go his way. Nevertheless they knew that in stronger hands the force of the law would soon encompass them, so while they could still do so they "pulled their freight."

One morning, with his remaining brothers and Doc Holliday at his side, Wyatt Earp, the six-shooter boss of Tombstone, rode slowly out of town, shaking hands with a few friends, waving an occasional farewell, his gleaming eyes daring any of his enemies to make one threatening move. The entire party carried rifles across their saddles and pistols in their belts. No sheriff, certainly not Johnny Behan dared molest them.

They had a modicum of excitement on their journey. They encountered, quite by accident, that unforgiving cowboy mentioned earlier in this chronicle, Mr. Curly Bill, and his gang. Curly's and Wyatt's guns dropped on each other at the same moment, but Wyatt shot first and "spattered Curly's brains all over the desert." Some people say Finn Clanton also checked out in this encounter.

Fifteen years later the "terrible skeleton," Doc Holliday, the fastest gunman, many persons believe, that the Southwest ever knew, died in Colorado of tuberculosis. Virgil Earp died in Nevada in 1905. James Earp died in California in 1926. Warren, the youngest brother, returned to Arizona and was shot to death in Willcox during a quarrel over a card game.

Wyatt, the old bull of the herd, the grandiose gentleman who could roar a terrible bluff and back it up with deadly pistols, succumbed again to bonanza fever and turned up in Alaska during the Klondike rush. Later he drifted through Nevada to take a look at Tonopah and finally peacefully died, aged eighty, in his home near Los Angeles. So passed the nerviest, the fightingest, and probably the cleanest clan of gunmen ever to redden the pages of western history.

But what finally became of that opposing leader, Ike Clanton, who threatened with such vehemence and whose back was such a familiar sight when gunplay broke out? Alas, poor Ike, he fell off his horse dead one morning. It seems he had stolen some cattle, and when two deputies accosted him, tradition held. They had no alternative save to shoot him right between the shoulder blades![1]

---

[1] The arguments over Tombstone's history are endless. Evidence recently unearthed, for instance, indicates that it may not have been Wyatt Earp who defended Johnny O'Rourke so dramatically, yet there are old-timers who swear it was Wyatt. This is the way the people love to hear the story told; this is the version from our folklore.

THE STOLEN SISTERS

The premonition of doom must surely have traveled with Mr. and Mrs. Royse Oatman, for they had already encountered grave dangers, and they had been repeatedly warned against this particular journey. They had elected to cross the two hundred miles of semi-desert from the village of Pimole to Fort Yuma on the southwestern frontier. The journey would have been hazardous even for a strong wagon train with military escort. But the Oatman family traveled alone.

What happened, therefore, was inevitable. It was, moreover, symbolic of the era, of the march of empire which seems ever to have been accompanied by tragedy and bloodshed. The Oatman episode was not the greatest drama in the Indian conquest, and not necessarily the most tragic; but it was the one that most inflamed people everywhere, commanding first regional then national attention—doubtless because the central figures were lovely Olive Oatman and her little sister, Mary Ann. Their true story became the best-selling book of its day. In their memory a thriving mountain town bears the Oatman name.

Young Lorenzo Oatman first saw the danger that day and touched his father's arm.

"Ho-o-o-o-o!" the father halted his two oxen, then spoke to his wife, "There is a movement yonder, half a mile ahead."

It could be nothing but Indians, they knew. This two-hundred-mile stretch held less than a dozen white people at the time. Later the expanse would be named Arizona Territory, but in 1851 it was still part of the New Mexico Territory, which had just lately been acquired from the nation to the south. Mr. Oatman tried futilely to calm his family's fears.

The Indians came boldly up to the group beside the wagon and stared rather insolently. Mr. Oatman waited for them to speak first.

"Tobacco," one of them finally demanded in Spanish.

Mr. Oatman, who spoke some Spanish, promptly filled a pipe, puffed it once, and passed it to them. It was a solemn gesture of peace, which meant nothing but to which the white people clung in frantic hope.

"Give us food," was the next demand.

Mr. Oatman demurred at that. The family was on half-rations already. And he had seventy-five miles more to go.

"Give us food!" the leader roared, ignoring the protests.

Mrs. Oatman produced a cake of heavy bread, all the prepared food available.

For the next ten minutes the Indians conferred among themselves, talking loudly in their own tongue. Mr. Oatman knew them to be Apaches, fiercest of all southwestern tribes, but he could understand nothing of their language. He reasoned that his safest course was to try to handle the situation with diplomacy rather than force.

He and his wife were the only adults in his party. His oldest son, Lorenzo, was fifteen, and Olive was sixteen. The other children were Lucy, Royce (spelled so in the records to distinguish him from his father, Royse), C. A., Mary Ann, and a baby—nine in all. Mr. Oatman knew that the two guns they could bring into action would not withstand any sort of attack.

To keep from revealing her abject fear, Mrs. Oatman was rearranging some of their possessions in the wagon. Olive, the oldest girl, was standing on the opposite side. Little Mary Ann was holding the rope that controlled the oxen.

The other children were sitting on the ground, and Mr. Oatman was watching the Indians from a point near a rear wagon wheel.

"Suddenly, as a clap of thunder from a clear sky, a deafening yell broke upon us, the Indians jumping into the air, uttering the most frightful shrieks, and at the same time springing toward us flourishing their war clubs which hitherto had been concealed under their wolf-skins." (The exact words are on record.)

Lorenzo Oatman was struck on the head. He sank to his knees but rose again. As he stood up, the boy saw a yelling savage grab Olive and drag her away from the wagon. He saw the mother run to her youngest baby, and then—oblivion. The murderous attack had taken place on top of a rocky bluff, some time in midafternoon. When Lorenzo Oatman regained consciousness, a full moon was gleaming in his face.

His efforts to rise were halted by extreme pain, and he never knew how long it took him to get to his hands and knees. Blood was scattered all around him, but he saw no sign of his family and no evidence of Indians, though memory of the attack surged back strong.

He looked around and presently saw the family wagon silhouetted on top of a bluff some twenty feet above him. Evidently he had been thrown or kicked over the rocky edge and left for dead.

He climbed up to the wagon, to find appalling proof of the tragedy. The mutilated bodies of his mother, father, brothers, and sisters lay there—all but Olive and Mary Ann. These two girls were nowhere to be found. The wagon had been ransacked. The oxen were missing, as was everything else of value. Fifteen-year-old Lorenzo was almost crazed with terror and pain. He did not know where to go; yet he could not just sit there and stare at death. So he started walking.

The family hadn't traveled far beyond the Gila River, which Lorenzo remembered crossing. He now waded it again in the darkness, and its water refreshed him and cleansed his wounds. He walked on. Toward dawn he encountered a pack of wolves, but they did not harm him. Near the next midday he realized that he would die of hunger if he didn't find help soon.

Aid came unexpectedly. He was terrified to see two Indians, mounted this time, coming toward him. The Indians had bows and arrows and might easily have slain him. But they proved to be friendly hunters, not of the Apache tribe. They carried him safely back to the white village from which the Oatmans had started their journey.

Lorenzo Oatman had already experienced more dangers and hardships than the average person encounters in a lifetime, and at fifteen he was decidedly precocious in outdoor craft and was in excellent health. Without his extraordinary stamina he would never have withstood the Indians' war-club blows nor the long trek back to civilization.

Alone and penniless in the small village, Lorenzo attracted much attention and sympathy. The focal point of all discussions, of course, was the fact that his two sisters, Olive and Mary Ann, had apparently been taken away as captives by the Apaches. This possibility prompted Lorenzo to beg for an expedition to rescue his sisters.

Sympathy, however, was all that he could be given. The white settlers there feared for their own lives. To arm some fifty men and start into the wild, unmapped hills would be suicidal, they declared. There was no use risking more lives to rescue two.

It was sound reasoning from their standpoint, but it did not quiet Lorenzo. Fury and longing filled the lad—whose experiences had matured him young. He resolved then and there to devote the remainder of his life, if necessary, to a search for his sisters. He did, in fact, become a "detective" such as no other man ever became in the wilderness West. His persistence and ingenuity are still cited as evidence of heroic devotion.

Another party of travelers came through the village and offered to take Lorenzo on to Fort Yuma, his family's original destination. He went with them—braving the same hazardous journey as before—and revisited the site of the massacre. The bones of the dead were buried, but no trace of Olive and Mary Ann was found.

In Fort Yuma, Lorenzo went at once to Commander Heinzelman.

"Will you send a troop of soldiers, sir, to hunt for my sisters?" he asked the commander.

The records now available of the commander's reply may be biased; at any rate, the answer was no. Lorenzo had built great hope on this source of aid. It had been suggested by adult friends. Fort Yuma had soldiers enough, but the government had assigned them strict duties. A tale of horror related by a mere boy bore little weight with the officials, even though Fort Yuma citizens were deeply concerned.

"Your sisters have probably been killed by this time," the officers assured the boy.

"But they weren't killed with the others!"

"Well, the redskins just wanted to torture them and kill them that night, probably, son. That's Apache fashion, you know."

"No!" Lorenzo insisted. "Other Indians, friendly Pimas, say they have heard rumors of two white captives in the Apache camps."

The officers smiled in what they fancied was kindness and wisdom.

"Hardly," one of them said. "Of what value would two mere girls be as captives? Especially one just seven?"

Lorenzo saw that it was hopeless to argue with soldiers. He told his story to miners, prospectors, and others who drifted in. Considerable speculation and interest was aroused after a few weeks, and finally a group of men met one night and discussed the matter thoroughly. Other rumors bearing out the reported captivity of the girls had sifted in by then. The men armed themselves and took provisions, determined to set out on a rescuing expedition. But the soldiery stepped in again.

"No," said the commander firmly. "It cannot be permitted. To begin with, all we have to go on is the yarn of a scared boy. Second, you are not strong enough in numbers and equipment to make the long trip that would be necessary. You would have to go two hundred miles or more from the fort. You would all be ambushed and killed."

Lorenzo's disappointment was almost unbearable. A Dr. Hewit had more or less adopted him, giving him clothing and a place to stay. The doctor was so angered by the commander's refusal that he took the boy with him to San Francisco, where he hoped to organize a party of volunteers for the search.

Soon after, however, Dr. Hewit was called to the East on a personal matter, and Lorenzo Oatman was left in San Francisco alone. The coast city at that time was gold-mad; everything centered around the fabulous wealth to be taken from the near-by streams. No one could be interested in the boy's tale of horror. Lorenzo found employment easily enough, but he made no friends. He was too morose.

"Often I strolled out onto the sidewalks," he wrote later, "and on into the hills, to the late hour of night, stung by thinking and reflecting upon the past and present of our family kingdom."

Constantly his mind held to the one absorbing desire—to find Olive and Mary Ann. This distraction interfered with his work, for he was injured and lost his job. He then went to work in the near-by mines. He felt that in time he might save enough money to hire an expedition. One night he told his tragic story to a group of hard miners in the camp where he worked. They listened attentively for a while.

"Haw-haw-haw!" they roared, when he was done.

His heart-rending narrative had been mistaken for a yarn and nothing more. Every subsequent effort he made to tell it in the mines met with incredulity and scoffing. In his anxiety he left his job and went with a party of travelers to Los Angeles, hoping to arouse some interest there. This was in October, 1854, three years after the massacre.

The three years had added stature and strength to Lorenzo Oatman. In Los Angeles he told his story with better results. A man is believed when a boy is not; Lorenzo at eighteen appeared almost a man. Moreover, in Los Angeles he heard some news. Travelers to the Coast via Fort Yuma verified his story.

"They are saying in Yuma," one new arrival declared, "that two girls by the name of Oatman were captured a while back, and one of them is still living with the Mohaves, away to the north of there."

This rumor brought both hope and sorrow to Lorenzo—and some confusion. Olive and Mary Ann had been captured by Apaches. Conceivably the girls had been sold to the Mohave tribe. But if just one were mentioned now, the other girl must have died.

It was also reported to Lorenzo that a Mr. Grinnell had come to Fort Yuma, had become interested in the fate of the Oatman family, and was now actively trying to organize a rescue party. Lorenzo's hope soared again. But he had no money beyond day-to-day needs, and Fort Yuma was nearly three hundred miles from Los Angeles. Then he learned that a party of miners was being organized to travel eastward across California to prospect in an area reputedly rich with gold. They would go almost to the Colorado River. Fort Yuma was on the Colorado, and although it was farther south, Lorenzo joined the party hoping to go somewhere near the Mohave Indian country at least.

Meanwhile, he told his story again and again, with all the force that a stalwart young man could command. People believed him. Many of the men had by now heard the same story from other sources. Lorenzo had a plan in mind, and he carefully developed it. He hoped to convert the prospecting party into an expedition to rescue the girls, or at least to learn their fate. But he couldn't pay the men for such an expedition, and it would be necessary to sell them on the idea as a volunteer move.

He almost succeeded. The party actually crossed the Colorado River into Arizona, but when the time came to go into the dangerous Indian country, their bravery subsided. Stories of Indian atrocities were too frightening. Lorenzo sank again into despair.

Back in Los Angeles, he next joined a surveying party which was heading for the same general area. Under strict government regulation, this party could not leave its assigned duties, but Lorenzo was permitted to do some scouting on his own.

"He took great risks," it is recorded. "He would outfit himself and travel alone to distant Indian villages, not knowing whether they would be friendly or otherwise. But he learned conflicting facts concerning Olive's fate, and so accomplished nothing. Everywhere, praise God, it was said that she was alive, but that was all. The Apaches had traded her to the Mohaves. The Mohaves were somewhere else."

Lorenzo joined at least two other surveying groups with no important results, then finally went again to Fort Yuma in 1855. By chance a letter had been left there for him by a

Mr. Rowlit, saying little but verifying reports that Olive still lived. Rowlit had been in the Indian country himself and had authentic news of a captive girl. Only one girl was mentioned now, and she was described as a grown woman. Lorenzo deduced that Mary Ann must have died or been killed.

His next move was to prepare a full statement of his case and send it to the *Los Angeles Star*. The newspaper published it "with some well-timed and stirring remarks." During the past four years the Oatman story had begun to spread all over the West, and Lorenzo's published letter now aroused great interest.

Soon thereafter a Mr. Black came to Los Angeles from Fort Yuma with more news.

"The Mohave Indian chief sent a messenger to Fort Yuma," Black reported, "and offered to sell two white girls to the commander of the fort. The price wasn't high, but the commander refused."

The *Star* published this information, and indignation soared. The only excuse the commander gave was that he couldn't afford to be obligated to an enemy chieftain and that he didn't believe the story about the captive girls anyway. Any payment sent the chief would simply have been stolen, the commander feared, and the army would have become the laughingstock of the country.

Lorenzo then drew up a petition, which was signed by a great number of citizens, imploring the governor of California to outfit men and horses for a rescue party. In a letter dated January 29, 1856, Governor J. Neely Johnson replied that the laws of California prevented him from providing the "men or means to render this needful assistance" and referred Lorenzo to the Indian department of the federal government.

Other newspapers had reached the coast cities by then, and they had taken up the interest in the Oatman tragedy. Some of Lorenzo's friends had voluntarily paid for advertisements, offering a reward for any authentic information about the Oatman sisters that might lead to their rescue. If Lorenzo could have approached these generous friends individually, doubtless he would have raised enough money to outfit an expedition. On the other hand, he was not sure now that a purely military expedition would do any good.

"If a strong force of men invaded the Mohave villages," his friends counseled, "the first thing the reds would do would be to drive a tomahawk in Olive's brain. You might kill all the reds, but they'd kill her first."

This advice seemed logical in light of the Indian customs of the day. Lorenzo wanted to go in alone and try to buy the girls' freedom, or go with a small party and try to negotiate a purchase, even at the tremendous risk involved. In Los Angeles, Lorenzo prepared a long presentation—as Governor Johnson had suggested—to be sent to Washington on the next boat bound for the East coast. He would have to wait months, of course, maybe a year, for a reply. And official Washington had grave troubles of another sort then; the Civil War was in the offing. Meantime, Lorenzo decided to take up a private collection and go alone into the Mohave country, starting from Fort Yuma. Such a trip would cost very little.

He headed north, staying within range of the known watercourses for protection from thirst. Most of the time he traveled at night for the excellent reason that enemies would not spot him so readily. By day he slept in a cave, under an overhanging rock, or in any dense and protected shade he could find. He had learned much trail craft from older men in the previous prospecting and surveying parties.

The region he traversed was so rugged as to defy description, beautiful in color and form, yet dangerous to one unaccustomed to it.

Lorenzo had an Indian guide for a part of the journey. His plan then was to go alone to the camp of a sub-chieftain known to be friendly to the whites and to try through him to open negotiations with the Mohaves who held Olive. Failing that, he was desperate enough to try to slip into the Indian camp at night and rescue Olive singlehanded. The latter course would have been worse than foolish, and fortunately he was spared from the necessity of attempting it.

In spite of his vigilance when traveling alone, one day Lorenzo was detected by three Indians. They tried to slip up on him, but he was alert and ready. The Indians crept very close. Lorenzo rose and fired at the right moment, and probably killed one. The others then rushed him, and Lorenzo fled. But for the cover of rocks to dodge behind, he would almost certainly have been killed. He kept on running, dodging, pausing for breath when he could, and shooting back when he had a glimpse of a target.

He feared that other Indians might have heard the shooting and come to aid their brethren. By luck, though, he reached the Colorado River soon after nightfall. He swam into the river, clung to a limb, and escaped his pursuers by following the swift current downstream. Later he fashioned a crude raft and eventually drifted, half-starved, down to Fort Yuma.

After this failure, Lorenzo went to The Monte, a town some 250 miles away in California. He was in search of work, though he was so full of despair that he would have been of little value to any employer. Two days after he had reached The Monte, a friend rode up to him on the street, handed him a copy of the *Los Angeles Star*, and pointed to a headline which read:

An American Woman Rescued from the Indians!

In just twenty-two more words, the dispatch reported that Olive Oatman had been rescued from the Mohaves and was now at Fort Yuma!

Lorenzo was almost crazed with hope and joy. He hardly dared believe it. Friends helped him obtain pack animals and equipment, and one of them accompanied him on the slow trek back to Fort Yuma. His long search was at last ended.

There was much yet to learn when he reached the fort. In the style of the newspaper reporters of that period, "it is best to draw a kindly veil over the actual meeting of Olive and Lorenzo," for after all it was a deeply emotional scene. One earnest witness wrote that "language was not made to give utterance to the feelings that rise, and swell, and throb through the human bosom upon such a meeting as this"; and the Reverend R. B. Stratton testified that "for nearly one hour not one word could either Olive or Lorenzo speak."

In time, though, Olive's entire narrative was heard again and again. The girl herself had changed incredibly. Very beautiful when Lorenzo had last seen her, she came back to him with her face disfigured by crude Indian tattooing. Her chin was hideously marked, and her body was covered with scars.

Her story (which is on record to the last harrowing detail) was told and retold throughout southern California and spread rapidly to the cities on the Coast, and finally to the East. It was the thriller headline of that day, just as it subsequently became a sensational best seller as a book.

Olive and Mary Ann had been forced to witness the

brutal murder of their parents, brothers, and sisters in that first attack on their wagon.

"I saw a savage strike Lorenzo with a club," Olive said. "When Lorenzo tried to arise, he was struck again, twice. To be sure he was dead, Lorenzo was kicked over the embankment. Thank God he was strong and was spared to us."

Held by the murderous Apaches, she and Mary Ann watched the bodies mutilated, the wagon ransacked. Then they were forced to walk away carrying burdens. Innumerable times the white girls were beaten with sticks and whips. They had almost nothing to eat for days, and their feet were soon bloody and raw from walking barefoot. The two reached the Indians' home camp in a virtual coma, after crawling part of the way, Olive testified.

Their first year of captivity was marked by routine cruelties. The two girls were forced to do every menial task. They lived on the scantiest fare—nuts, roots, and wild beans; meat was denied them. Often they were tortured solely for the entertainment of the Indian women and children.

Little Mary Ann, who had been just seven, was so weakened by mistreatment and especially by hunger that she eventually died. Olive buried her and kept many a lonely vigil beside the grave. Tiring of her after some months, the Apaches traded Olive to the Mohaves for a few trinkets. But she fared no better there—indeed, she found that the Mohaves had even less to eat than the Apaches. Her constant prayer was either for deliverance or for death. Of course, she thought all members of her family were dead.

Despite Lorenzo's repeated efforts, her rescue finally came about through the untiring efforts of a kindly stranger. Mr. Grinnell, who has been mentioned earlier, was a mechanic stationed at Fort Yuma three years after the Oatman massacre. He became interested in the fate of Olive and Mary

Ann and was so angered by the commandant's refusal to give Lorenzo aid that he undertook the girls' rescue as a personal project. He learned in time that the little girl had died, but he persisted in his efforts to find Olive.

His procedure was to offer a reward for Olive's return. This had also been tried by Lorenzo, through many newspaper announcements paid for by sympathetic citizens. But Mr. Grinnell wisely offered the reward where it would do the most good. He spoke constantly of it, not to the white people, but to the Indians who came frequently to the fort. His reward was offered not in money but in horses, clothing, food, and other articles the Indians could use.

Nothing came of his efforts for a long while, then one day at 4 P.M., the fort cannons boomed out, men shouted from the parapets, rifles cracked, flags were waved, and all the residents and soldiery came running.

To everybody's amazement, a friendly Yuma Indian named Francisco, who lived near the fort, had come to claim the reward. The intrepid fellow had walked nearly four hundred miles round-trip, endangered his life, and out-bargained the Mohaves to acquire "ownership" of Olive Oatman. He led her to Mr. Grinnell and calmly waited for his pay.

Grinnell did not have the reward ready, but it was gathered with great haste, and Francisco was given more than he had expected. In time, the Indian became a local chieftain because of the fame the exploit brought him.

Olive relived her terrible experiences each time she told her story, so as quickly as he could Lorenzo arranged to take her away. Her brother planned to move with her into Oregon, where far from the scene of the tragedy she could perhaps find partial forgetfulness. She had been through unspeakable tortures and sufferings and had been delivered almost miraculously. In Oregon her failing health would be restored, and only the ugly tattoo marks on her chin would remain to show of her captivity. In Oregon the brother and sister could start life anew.

But Fate was still not done with Olive Oatman. The girl brooded unceasingly. She and Lorenzo made money from the book written about them, and they attended school for six months in Santa Clara Valley, California. But Olive's melancholia grew steadily worse, and on March 5, 1858, Lorenzo sailed with her from San Francisco on the steamship "Golden Age" and arrived in New York several months later. Even the sea voyage did not help her. She remained in the East, where she eventually died insane.

5

ESCAPE FROM THE GHOST HOLE

Pow!

Train engineer Bill Harper was suddenly tense. That could have been a gunshot. The train was climbing through Pantano Canyon, where the narrow rock walls made crazy echoes, and he had the engine cab tight against the night storm. Even the belching of the stack was now a muffled *poom-poom-poom-poom* rhythm which he felt rather than heard.

He strained to see better. His headlight made a huge halo in the rain out front. He opened a window, taking the storm full in the face. *Pow!* The noise came again, and Mr. Harper saw a red spot in the halo.

"Trouble!" he yelled at Greer, his fireman. "Red light!" He knew now that those explosions had been rail torpedoes. He was braking down as quickly as he could. The red flare was only a few yards away. Washout, maybe. He leaned far out, squinting, as the train stopped short. He reached beside his cab seat for a pistol: a man had to expect anything in this Arizona wilderness of 1884.

"All right!" a voice shouted then. "Put yore hands up, Harper! And you, Greer!"

The command was backed by strong profanity. Harper couldn't see anybody, but in quick fury he shot at the voice. The shot was answered by a fusillade. Harper collapsed and hung limply, his hands hanging outside the window. Greer

71

crouched near the firebox until a masked bandit climbed dripping and cursing into the cab.

By this time, too, things were happening in the express car immediately behind the engine. Expressman and guard both knew the train carried a large shipment of money. They heard the shouting. The guard, Travis L. Collins, drew his gun and ran to peer out. For a moment his face was framed in a little glass window.

Crack! Crack! In the interior light Collins had made a too-perfect target. He crumpled and died right there.

"My God!" breathed the expressman. He knew what was afoot now. Common sense told him he would be foolish to resist. But he did rush to the doors and lock them, then take some leather bags from the safe. The bags were heavy. He looked frantically around. There stood a lighted stove. He opened the door and crammed in four bags. Even if gold melts, it's still gold. He kicked the stove door shut.

The bandits were not prone to argue. They planted a stick of powder under the front of the car and touched it off. The explosion joined in the thunder of the storm. One whole corner of the car was torn away. Two armed masked men climbed in. The expressman had crouched behind a desk at the far end of the car and was unhurt. On command, he opened the safe. In scarcely five minutes the two raiders had passed out leather bags, had warned the expressman to make no move, and had disappeared on horses into the stormy night.

The total money in that shipment was $62,000. A count of the stove contents showed approximately $12,000. Thus the loot, plus the two murders and the damaged car, made this one of the major robberies of the whole wild-west era. It had been committed by men who were obviously both experienced and fearless and who, because of the rain, were lucky as well. No hint of a trail was left by them.

The holdup occurred about 11 P.M., and it was well past midnight before Sheriff R. N. Leatherwood in Tucson could be notified. By dawn he had gathered a posse of six men and horses. A special engine and freight car ran them out to Pantano Canyon thirty-odd miles away. The rain had stopped. The armed men led their horses out of the freight car and mounted.

"Thing to do," the sheriff said then, "is to figure which way they would've went, and how far."

"They'd head for the border, wouldn't they?" a member of the posse suggested.

"Nope, I believe not. That's a guess they'd expect us to make. But they'd know they left no trail. They'd know they weren't recognized. They'd have trouble with so much American money in Mexico—invite suspicion. I bet they go to some town. We can spread the news and watch who begins spending lots of money. But we'll ride first."

"Which way, sheriff?"

"Well, they'd have to go northwest from here. In a canyon. Black night, raining, thorny cactus—we won't need a trail to follow them for a few miles, anyway."

That was sound deduction. As he rode along, Sheriff Bob Leatherwood did some more thinking. Four men could ride only so far before they would need fresh horses. If the men were fleeing in the rain at night—

"There's four or five ranches around," he said, an hour later. "Let's go first to Nigger Beard's."

"Why Nigger's?" asked a posseman.

"They'd figure to bulldoze a nigger quicker'n a white man, wouldn't they?"

Nigger Beard was a humble black rancher-farmer named Walter Beard. He was well liked around Tucson and "Nigger" was an affectionate nickname. When the posse came to his door, well after sunrise, Bob Leatherwood eyed him shrewdly.

73

"Why ain't you out working, Nigger?" he asked.

"Naw suh, I don't feel so well today."

"H'mmmm." Nigger's eyes did look somewhat abnormal—too wide. "You had any callers, Nigger?"

"Naw suh, not none, Mr. Bob. You all knows you is welcome, though."

"Thanks, we'll rest our horses a bit, while we visit."

The sheriff walked out to Nigger's corral. One side of it was bound by a rock cliff some twenty feet high, which extended past the fence ends two or three miles off into the desert. Nigger's corral was empty.

A scant quarter-mile away the sheriff found a horse. It was huddled against the cliff, head down. The sheriff edged closer. Plainly the horse was sick and covered with dried sweat. The cliff had protected it from the last rain showers, which would otherwise have washed off the sweat. Then the sheriff climbed the cliff. A half-mile or so away he saw two more horses, standing as if exhausted. He came back to the house then.

"Nigger," he began anew, "I like you. Now I'd hate to have to beat hell out of a man I like. Start talking, Nigger!"

"Mr. Bob, don't mistreat me, suh! I doesn't want to git myself killed! You all white gentlemens—!"

"You won't get killed. I'm a sheriff. But there's half-dead horses out there, one still sweaty, and your own horses aren't in sight. Now, who were they—and which way did they go? Talk!"

Nigger talked.

Yes suh, he knew the men. They had swore to come back and slit his throat if he did talk, but he had to tell Mr. Bob.

"It was Mr. Ned McClosky, one of 'em," Nigger said. "He done slap me aroun'. And Mr. Vaughn. And—"

"John Vaughn?"

"Yes suh, him. And Mr. Od'n. And a greaser man."

74

"H'mmm! Know the Mexican's name?"

"They calls him Pete, suh."

One of the possemen had a hunch. "Probably Pete Garfías. Pedro Garfías. He's a hell-snorter. He'd do it, all right."

"They took your horses, Nigger?" the sheriff demanded further.

"Yes suh, Mr. Bob. And they headed for the Ghos' Hole."

"Yeah? They say so?"

"Not to me, suh. But Mr. Od'n argued it. They was some drunk."

Od'n. That would be Odom. And southern Arizona held only one Odom, F. J. Odom, a miner-loafer-gambler. He'd fit in with a bandit gang, all right.

In fact it all fitted together now in the sheriff's mind. McClosky, Vaughn, Pete Garfías, and F. J. Odom. A likely quartet of murderers. And if honest Nigger Beard said they had headed toward the Ghost Hole—

He gave Nigger five dollars and told him to keep the bandits' horses for his own. Then he led his six possemen toward a little-known spot on the slope of a mountain, no more than a hole among a cluster of rocks. Four of the possemen hadn't even known of its existence. For their benefit, Leatherwood explained that it was a cave around which ignorant Mexicans and people like Nigger Beard had built superstitious legends. An old Spanish *conquistador* was supposed to live in the hole, a man who had come there three hundred years ago and had found a stream of eternal life underground.

"The ghosts we find, if any, won't be three hundred years old," the sheriff said. "Come to think of it, it's a good place, if they meant to hide."

"No place for anybody to live in any length of time,"

75

one posseman argued. "I bet they were just lying, to throw Nigger off."

"Then how about these tracks in the mud?" asked the sheriff, pointing. "They've only been sprinkled on."

Sure enough, the tracks of four horses showed now, ahead of the posse—tracks obviously made just before the rain had stopped early that morning.

Approaching the Ghost Hole a while later, the seven officers deployed, rifles in hand. "No need to take chances," Mr. Leatherwood warned sensibly. He himself led the way. They saw horses, hobbled and grazing down the slope. Nigger Beard's horses.

"They're here, all right!" cried the sheriff, elated. "But they wasn't expecting us. Maybe I can slip up close and—"

His words were like a signal. A rifle shot sounded from the cave mouth.

The sheriff's horse reared, screamed once, and fell. Leatherwood narrowly escaped a broken leg. He had to shoot his animal in the head to end its suffering.

Meantime, his possemen answered that first shot. They dismounted to seek cover, then literally poured bullets at the black dot which was the entrance to Ghost Hole.

"See anybody?" the sheriff shouted. "Give 'em hell!"

The bandits were safely crouched behind rocks, however, and were evidently well armed. They fired back rapidly. One posseman, a Tucson cattleman named Follett, was struck in the ribs and crawled bleeding down hill. The remaining six then lay prone and took no chances. For half an hour or so the exchange of bullets kept up, but if either side made any more hits, the other side couldn't know of it. Finally Mr. Leatherwood changed his plan. He cupped his hands to shout orders.

"Back down out of range, men! No reason to get hurt. We know where they are, and we can starve them out."

That made good sense. It would be far cheaper in the long run to keep a watchful siege rather than to try to storm the place.

Two riders were sent to take the wounded man back home. They were also to arrange for further help so the siege could be handled easily in shifts.

With considerable courage, since he had to expose himself at several points, Sheriff Leatherwood crawled closer to the mouth of the cave and shouted out his plan to the bandits.

"We'll keep you here all spring if we have to! Come on out with your hands up and you won't be hurt."

"Go to hell!" came the answer, supplemented with much derisive profanity. Mr. Leatherwood backed away.

The officers planted themselves in such a way that they could shoot down any man who tried to escape. They expected an attempt at night, but the bandits' luck failed them, for the rain came no more and the night skies were clear and moonlit. No more shots were fired, and no sign of the bandits was seen after the first day's shooting. Apparently the four men had elected to crouch down in the Ghost Hole and live with the ghosts.

By the sixth day the silent siege had become routine, and news of it had spread through southern Arizona. Many men rode out voluntarily to stand watch and to talk and look on. Here was a peculiar situation indeed. Bets were placed on when the bandits would surrender and on whether or not they would finally elect to fight their way out. By now most of the sheriff's helpers hoped they would fight it out.

On the eighth day a cowboy rode somewhat hurriedly up to the tent that had been set up as official field headquarters. He asked for Mr. Leatherwood.

"Sheriff," he began, "I heard a Mexican say he seen Pete Garfías and Ned McClosky over in Nogales day before yesterday."

77

The sheriff was thunderstruck. He couldn't believe it, but the cowboy was insistent. Moreover, the cave had shown no sign of life in a long time.

"I'll find out," Mr. Leatherwood announced solemnly.

He would allow no one to accompany him. With two drawn pistols he crept toward the cave entrance. Then slowly but boldly he stood up and called out.

"Hey in there, I got a deal to offer." No one answered.

The sheriff went forward, guns ready. Stepping slowly, eyes alert for the slightest hint of movement among the rocks, he approached the place. Again he called, and again he had no answer. Presently the waiting possemen saw him actually disappear inside, and they all ran up, rifles in hand. They met the sheriff coming out.

78

"Not a danged sign of 'em!" he cried in dismay. "They've give us the slip, else they're holed in way down deep."

"They ain't come out this way, I'd swear to that," somebody said. Others nodded emphatic agreement, and Mr. Leatherwood knew that to be true.

"All right," said he. "Git some torches."

Twelve men then formed a strange procession that filed down the mysterious entrance to the Ghost Hole. Not one of them had ever been in here before. They were like ghosts themselves, their shadows dancing on crystalline walls. They crept along, alert to any danger, straining to see or hear whatever the cavern might reveal. The very size of the place soon awed them.

They found rooms as big as barns. Moreover, there seemed to be no end of passages, hallways, holes, and rooms. Gigantic stalagmites stood everywhere, and stalactites resembling icicles one inch to twenty feet long draped the high ceilings. In the flickering light of pine torches these underground formations made the place a fantasy land. Bat dung formed a carpet on the floor of the cave, and ugly bats flitted everywhere. Ghosts? Ghosts indeed! The white men were almost ready to believe the wildest yarns people such as poor Nigger Beard had long been telling.

But Sheriff Leatherwood was a realist. "Here's where they've been, all right," he said, pointing to tracks and other signs of the bandits' occupancy. "Only one thing we know now—there's another way out of here. I think I know how to find it. Come on."

Outside again, he posted men at vantage points all around the mountain, then he and one helper took armloads of wood back into the cave. As far down as they could conveniently go, they built a fire.

In less than an hour a man outside shouted, "There's smoke! Tell Bob smoke's coming out!"

Smoke had revealed what the posse had not found—a hole in the side of the mountain opposite the known entry-way. It proved to be only a chimney-like crack effectively hidden by rocks and mesquite growth on the outside, but the signs made it plain that the bandits had escaped here. Sheriff Leatherwood and his posse had no alternative but to ride on back to Tucson. They endured the grinning faces of fellow citizens stoically. Of course, many faces were not grinning; murder and robbery were still unavenged.

It was said later that Sheriff Leatherwood did not sleep for nearly four days after that. F. S. Ingalls, later famous as a warden of Yuma Prison, happened to be in Tucson then, and he joined Bob Leatherwood in a further search. Ingalls and Leatherwood had wide acquaintances throughout the borderland, and while they were known to be officers, they managed to operate by employing help secretly.

One invaluable helper was a Mexican named Mendoza y Lillantino, who had cause to despise the bandit Pete Garfías. He came to Mr. Leatherwood in Nogales, where the officers hoped to get trace of Garfías.

"Pedro hear you have coom," Lillantino said, simply. "He iss go away. In Sonora he iss wanted too, so he run to thee heels."

The "heels" toward which he pointed were the Oro Blanco Mountains. Leatherwood and Ingalls quietly rode out. They could find no trail at first, but eventually Ingalls, circling wide, found tracks of two horses.

"That'll be him riding and leading a pack horse," the sheriff deduced. "He's prepared to hole in. He won't know he's being followed for a while, so if we hurry we can over-take him before night."

However, in the arid, open Arizona country, trailing a man for any length of time without being seen is an impos-sibility. Garfías doubtless knew by midafternoon that two men were pursuing him. He was then approaching the ruins of an old mining camp called Oro Blanco, so he elected to ambush them from behind an adobe house near the end of the single street. He had a rifle ready. But, unfortunately for Garfías, he was a little jittery and shot before the officers were in good range.

"Let's git him, Ingalls!" Leatherwood yelled, spurring and shooting as he rode. He stretched low near his horse's neck.

Together they literally rushed Pete Garfías to death. The Mexican shot repeatedly but missed. He was dead when the two officers came to him. They searched his possessions but found none of the money that had been stolen from the train.

That left McClosky, Odom, and Vaughn still at liberty, and McClosky had been reported seen at Patagonia, a few miles east. Sheriff Leatherwood stayed around Nogales, the Mexican border town, for several days. And again he quietly passed the word around, now offering a five-hundred-dollar reward, not in public notices, but by word of mouth in the town saloons and bawdyhouses. Almost immediately the offer bore fruit.

Just after midnight one Monday, the sheriff was in bed in his hotel room. The room was on the ground floor. He had blown out his lamp only ten minutes before, when he heard a whispered call at his window. He sat up instantly, unholstering his gun.

"Who is it?" he demanded.

"*Un amigo, Señor!* Sh-h-h-h!" A woman's voice pleaded, still whispering.

"Well?" Leatherwood asked, in a lower tone. He stayed in the shadows.

"Thee re-ward monee, Señor—I don't want heem, but I tell you sometheeng."

They talked for a few minutes, then the woman departed. The next day Sheriff Leatherwood announced publicly that the three remaining bandits had escaped into Mexico, and that he himself would go over there to get them. He outfitted his saddle and pack horses and headed south that afternoon.

Soon after nightfall, however, he did an about-face, traveling due northward, skirting the towns, and at first moving for the most part at night. After an arduous five-day trek he arrived in the Salt River Valley, and after waiting for the sun to go down he came into the new town of Phoenix.

In the past two weeks the sheriff had grown stubby whiskers, which changed his appearance some. He kept his star and his guns concealed and came into Phoenix quietly like a rancher or a miner. He knew the three fugitives by sight, and he wanted time to look around. He also knew that one of his men was an inveterate gambler, so he edged into the various gaming places on Washington and Montezuma streets. He saw no sign of his men.

Tired now to distraction, he eventually went to the Lemon Hotel for a rest. He knew Mr. and Mrs. Lemon, and after registering he partly confided in them. This was on Saturday night.

"You ain't had no suspicious looking guests, I reckon, Mrs. Lemon?" Mr. Leatherwood asked, wearily but in fun, cracking the standard joke of officers and hotel proprietors.

Mrs. Lemon didn't laugh with him, as she might have. She eyed him a moment, thinking. "You know," she said then, quietly, "I could say yes to that, Mr. Leatherwood."

Something in her tone caught his attention. "Why, ma'am? How you mean?"

"Five, six days ago, a trampy looking man come here. Wild-eyed, dirty. He took a room. I demanded cash because

I thought he'd be a bum. He got a little mad and dug out a pouch full of gold."

"That so?"

"He slept like a log for nearly twenty hours. Then he went out a while and come back dressed up fit to kill."

"H'mmmm! What name'd he give?"

"McIlvane. Says he's Scotch."

"McI— h'mmmm!" The sheriff was deeply interested now.

"He's over at the California House—you know it," Mr. Lemon put in. "There's a new girl there. She's milking his gold, I think."

"I'll walk over," the sheriff decided.

Mr. Lemon understood his intent. "You want I should go with you?"

"No, better not, if it's who I think. It's my job."

But Mr. Lemon went anyway, staying a reasonable distance behind his guest from Tucson. He carried a gun, just in case.

At the California House, Sheriff Leatherwood told the madam that "McIlvane sent for me." Genial and unwary, she bade him welcome and escorted him to an upstairs room. She opened the door. Three men and a few women were lounging there, with cards and liquor bottles at hand.

Mr. Leatherwood had his pistol in his hand, but he kept it concealed behind his big hat as he stood in the door. That would give him a chance to be sure of his ground. And he was sure instantly.

McClosky, alias McIlvane, recognized the sheriff first, despite his growth of whiskers. McClosky had been sitting on a table with one knee hooked up under his chin. With incredible swiftness he straightened out, lifting a pistol from his right boot leg as he did so.

Bang! Bang! The sheriff shot from belt position.

83

Women shrieked. The madam rushed back up the hall. Instantly, it seemed, the whole house was in an uproar. The other two men in the room with McClosky leaped through a window onto a sloping roof.

But there was no more shooting. McClosky hadn't been able to fire. When Mr. Lemon got there, Leatherwood was bending over the bandit making him talk. Lemon, the sheriff, and the bawdyhouse madam, heard his last words.

"I should've . . . stuck . . . with 'em," he lamented, in agony.

Leatherwood guessed what he meant. "Where'd they go, McClosky? Where's Vaughn? And Odom?"

"They're getting out . . . tonight. I should h've . . . went."

He died there on the floor. He had lingered in town for one more Saturday-night fling.

Down in Nogales he had two-timed a pretty Mexican girl, a señorita who wouldn't take two-timing. He had wanted the señorita to accompany him in his flight toward Phoenix, and when she couldn't go he had met up with another pretty Mexican girl and tried to take her. The first one had whispered word of all this to Sheriff Leatherwood. Later she got her five-hundred-dollar reward. McClosky wasn't the first man, nor the last, to wreck his plans by two-timing a woman. Only four thousand dollars or so in cash was found in McClosky's effects. Without stopping to get the sleep he now badly needed, Sheriff Leatherwood, assisted by a Phoenix officer named Novinger, made hurried calls on all the livery stables and stores in Phoenix and learned that two men had indeed outfitted themselves for travel on Saturday. Novinger elected to go with Leatherwood on the chase.

"No tellin' which way they went," Novinger said. He was primarily a farmer and was inexperienced as an officer.

But Sheriff Leatherwood was shrewd. "Well, human na-

84

ture's what it is. They know they done murder and robbery down south. They already fled this far north, and they'd naturally want to put still more miles between them and the scene."

Novinger nodded. "That's so. They could—look, I know some Indians, Maricopas, cutting ironwood in the Squaw Peak country. They'd see anybody on horseback."

It was a good hunch. Leatherwood and Novinger rode north to the Indians' camp before Sunday dawn, and three men said they had seen the riders yesterday. Two of the Indians were hired as trackers.

There was no rain to cover up tracks this time, and when the sun rose even the white officers could follow the trail easily as it led into rugged hills.

"They're headin' for the Verde Valley, or else Prescott," Mr. Novinger said, after an hour or so.

"And they don't know they're being chased now. They just moved on from Phoenix for safety, knowing McClosky was a show-off who'd get them in trouble sooner or later." Mr. Leatherwood was speculating. "And ain't these tracks right fresh?"

There was a low ridge dead ahead, a mountain saddle. An Indian topped it first. Suddenly he reined in, pointing. The sheriff spurred. Less than two hundred yards below was a camp! Here at 8 A.M. two men were belatedly cooking breakfast. They hadn't even caught up their horses, which were hobbled and grazing near by, so when they saw two whites and two Indians they just grabbed their guns and fled on foot.

"Halt!" Mr. Leatherwood yelled. "I'm giving you warning!"

They didn't halt, and they soon found fairly good cover in rocks. Both officers shot and missed, then had to duck for safety themselves.

But the strange running fight there on the rocky slope didn't last long. F. J. Odom was dropped with a rifle bullet through the forehead. John Vaughn managed to climb a low knoll which, incidentally, had a crumbled, prehistoric Indian ruin on top. There he crouched behind a rock wall for a few minutes. The wall made a breastwork shoulder high.

Crack! Crack! Crack! The hills reverberated with staccato rifle fire. Then Vaughn waved his hat.

"All right!" he yelled. "Don't shoot no more. I'm done!"

He stood up, on command, with hands high. His one pocketful of ammunition was gone.

At the trial and afterward, Vaughn swore he knew nothing of the money stolen from the train. He had been given only a few hundred dollars. McClosky had cached the main portion, said he. They had all agreed to lie low for three months, then meet quietly and split their wealth. Vaughn now decided that McClosky might have doublecrossed him and Odom. As for their fourth pal, Garfías, his death was good riddance, Vaughn felt. He was "only a Mexican" anyway, and he had been scared ever since the holdup.

John Vaughn, the last of the four bandits, was a very young man, handsome in a way, and even likable. This may have accounted for the surprising leniency shown him. People freely predicted he would be sentenced to death. Instead he was sentenced to life imprisonment in the old Territorial Prison at Yuma, an early-day hellhole which had many a notorious desperado on its guest list.

In actuality, Vaughn served only eighteen years. He was called a model prisoner. When he was finally pardoned in 1902, he came back to Tucson. He must have known, or guessed, that even then he was being shadowed. The bulk of that stolen $50,000 was still missing, and the express company hadn't forgotten it.

But after a week or so in Tucson, John Vaughn suddenly disappeared once more. The company detective hired to shadow him moved fast but not fast enough. Vaughn's trail led right back into the mountains to the Ghost Hole!

The place had acquired a new name during the intervening years—the Bandits' Den. A man, doubtless Vaughn, was seen entering the cave, but when the detective arrived there was no sign of him except a freshly dug hole deep inside the cave. Beside the hole were some empty leather bags, half-rotted but easily identified.

To this day Vaughn is still missing. How much money he got from the bandit cache is not known, and his strange case—in which both the law and the criminal won—is probably closed forever.[1]

[1] No accredited historian seems to have any proof of the authenticity of this story. Yet it appears again and again in folklore. Occasionally the names of the characters and the amount of money stolen vary somewhat, but there is a distinct similarity in the action in each version of the story. Moreover, the drama is typical of the period. It must be remembered that in the hectic frontier days very few current events were recorded; most of our best stories cannot now be documented.

The Ghost Hole, or Bandits' Den, is, of course, the Colossal Cave of our day, a popular tourist attraction. One version of the legend says that the loot was divided three ways, then buried in three separate places in the cave, and that Vaughn recovered only the third he knew about. Thus thousands of dollars in gold are perhaps still hidden there!

6

BARON OF THE BORDER

CONSIDER *the texture of our daydreaming. Any adult male among us is likely to drift toward romance. If we are normal, we dream of woman and we dream of wealth. We dress it all in the diaphanous fabric of improbability, and then, sensitive, we overdress it with the gossamer of glamour and yearning.*

Only so far do daydreams go for most of us, but not for Jim Reavis. Jim, to my belief, was the greatest southwesterner who ever lived—not one to be envied or emulated, but one to be looked upon with everlasting awe. He dreamed as you and I have dreamed, grandly, magnificently, unrestrainedly—and then, in the strangest circumstances in all our history, made every detail of his dreams come true.

"You know something?" he would say to his friends. "I'd like to quit my job and be important. I'm making six dollars a week. But I'd like to leave here and go down to the Mexican border country and get rich. I'd like to have a big hacienda with fine houses and horses and servants and all that. I'd like to have a span of milk-white horses for my own—perfectly matched stallions.

"And I'd like a gorgeous señorita *to ride behind them with me, a girl with black hair and a red shawl and little dancing feet, and me in a tight velvet suit with laced breeches, a serape over my shoulder and on my head a big sombrero*

*with gold braid. I'd like to take her traveling with me to call
on kings and princes and eat fine food and be entertained
everywhere in the finest homes. Yes, I'd like all that."*

*Who wouldn't, Jim, who wouldn't! You said that in the
eighteen seventies, when you were a mule driver in St.
Joseph, Missouri. Yet you put into words the golden pretense in every honest man's mind, now and evermore. How,
then, did you succeed when we cannot? What had you that
we lack? We speak in jest, you understand that; because, of
course, you ultimately let us down, and the dishonesty of it
all lay naked like a harlot's corpse. You hurt us more than
you can ever know. But even so, we read of you with last-
ing stimulation. We see justice done, see right triumph, see
reality in all its scientific exactitude, and still love you for
what you might have done. So compassionate are our God-
given imaginations.*

Jim spoke his dreams aloud to combat boredom and poverty,
while he jogged along behind the unromantic mules. He was
lately a deserter from the Civil War. Personable in every
way, he was charming as only an unscrupulous man can be.
Yet nobody took him seriously. "Whoops!" they would
shout, in answer to his grand talking. "Maybe we'll go with
you, Jim." But what Jim Reavis did about his dreams has
permanently colored the legend and lore of this sun-bathed
region. It is fantastic, it is unbelievable, it is fictional—but
every detail is documented by records of the United States
District Court.

One day Jim disappeared from his humble job in Missouri, leaving several unpaid debts. Nobody knew what
became of him, and in truth nobody much cared; in a very
short time he was forgotten.

Five years later a stately gentleman in a red velvet Spanish
costume appeared in Arizona with a beautiful wife and a

retinue of servants. Upon his arrival the following manifesto was published throughout the region:

AVISO!

Harken ye, all men. That person or persons now situated on *La Baronia de Arizonac*, known also as the Peralta Grant, will be subject to immediate removal unless proper arrangements be made and set forth as a matter of record.

By order of The Baron,
DON JAMES ADDISON
DE PERALTA-REAVIS.

The stately gentleman was Don James himself. He and his wife, dressed in the richest finery of old Spain, rode about the territorial towns in a shiny coach drawn by six milk-white horses. They announced that they had come to claim an ancestral barony, a great estate left to the baroness by her grandfather, who had traced his ownership directly to King Ferdinand of Spain. And how large was their barony, and where was it located? At that question the excitement began.

The "Barony of Arizona," as shown on an "official" map, was no mere rancho or suburban estate; it included all of twelve million acres. Rectangular in shape, the barony extended from a line just west of Phoenix, Arizona Territory, to Silver City, New Mexico, and embraced much of the most valuable land in the Southwest. All of the great Coronado Trail region, through the present Crook and Apache National Forests, was included, as well as most of the beautiful Tonto National Forest, with its famed Mogollon Rim stand of pine. Frontier citizens were just beginning to build cities and railroads, so the timber stand was very valuable.

The barony included every city, town, and village in Arizona of any importance, except Tucson. It included most of the rich mines from which people were taking fortunes in gold, copper, and silver. It included the best of the irrigable desert lands, several thousand acres of which had already been made productive with water from the Gila and Salt rivers. The barony also included much of the best cattle-grazing land.

Of course, the frontiersmen, being what they were—Americans all the way—roared in indignation.

"What does this poppycock mean?" a spokesman demanded of the sheriff one morning, in behalf of an armed committee. "Trying to kick us off our land!"

"Gentlemen, I'm sorry to say it ain't poppycock," the sheriff answered. "I wish it was. You all better come with me to the United States marshal." The marshal, the judge, and the land commissioner were called on to back up the sheriff.

"All that Don James Addison de Peralta-Reavis claims is true," they announced. "Federal investigators have dug into his inheritance. It is documented at every turn. The records are on file in the old monasteries of Mexico and Spain, showing that his wife did truly inherit this twelve million acres. And under the Treaty of Guadalupe Hidalgo, the United States has to recognize such land grants."

"Then that means we are all squatters!" the citizens howled.

"That's just what it amounts to. He can kick you off. But he's giving you the chance to stay—if you pay his fees."

Yes, the great baron was fair. If you were a poor man who cut crossties or hauled logs to the mill, his agents would charge you only five hundred dollars or so to keep your little cabin. But if you owned the sawmill itself, you might have to pay five thousand dollars. Suppose you were an important businessman and owned the railroad for which ties were cut on the barony and which had right of way there. In that case your fee was fifty thousand dollars—and Don James actually did collect that amount from the Southern Pacific Railroad.

He assessed a similar amount on the silver mines at Globe; he collected all the traffic would bear everywhere—and did it with such grace and skill that surprisingly little objection was raised. Of course, hardship resulted. Pioneers had very little cash, and many had to give up and move away. But the Don brought in new settlers who had the money to pay him. Many more had to sell cattle or mine stock to obtain the money, which soon began to pour into Don James's coffers.

The big corporations, such as the railroad and the mines, naturally fought back. They hired the most distinguished lawyers in the country to fight the baron. Among them were such impressive names as Roscoe Conkling, Collis P. Huntington, Charles Crocker, and Robert G. Ingersoll. These four, notably, investigated the baron's astounding claim, checked again the old monastery documents—it was a custom in the old days for Spain and Mexico to file official papers in monasteries—and tried to find a loophole with the aid of federal government investigators. But there was no loophole. The lawyers ended by taking Don James and his charming wife, Doña Sofia Loreto, into their homes to entertain them and, in behalf of their clients, court good will.

For a while, then, the baron and the baroness soared high. Twin sons were born to them, an event which caused a mild sensation in the Southwest. Soon the little boys were shown off to the public, dressed in gorgeous Spanish raiment as were mother and father. But, all told, the family really did not stay in the Southwest long at a time. They would come in, inspect the property, check up on the collection agents, let a few contracts, then disappear again. But they were much in evidence elsewhere in the world.

At St. Louis, Missouri, Don James purchased an expensive mansion. He and his family lived there as much as three months a year, for St. Louis was an up-and-coming city with gay social life. Because of his importance to the government—and its importance to him—he also purchased a fine home in Washington, D. C. Later he acquired a still more expensive estate in surburban Mexico City, where he spent the summer months in elegant idleness. When he and his wife tired of Mexico, they went to Madrid, Spain, and bought a fourth magnificent home.

The fame of the great *baron de Arizonac* had spread across the ocean, and he and the baroness were cordially welcomed in Madrid society. No less a personage than the American ambassador gave a state ball for them, which was attended by royalty. Records say that Don James "was easily the most distinguished looking gentleman present, tall, exquisitely dressed, perfect in grace and bearing and manner of speech."

Records reveal that he spent more than sixty thousand dollars a year on travel alone. This figure was substantiated later by his own statement. He would come to the United States and shuttle between Arizona, California, and Washington for months at a time, then go abroad again. Everywhere he went he made an impression. In the frontier towns of his barony he liked to attend festivals, especially Mexican *fiestas*, and—exactly as mule-driver Jim Reavis had dreamed in Missouri—dance with all the lovely señoritas. At one such village *fiesta* in Mexico a pretty little solo dancer entertaining him in the plaza fainted from the heat.

93

"Water! Water! Bring her water to drink!" the baron ordered, bending over her.

Water was unavailable near by, and someone had to run quite a long way to get it. The baron was furious. He revived the girl in due time—then donated five thousand dollars for a project to pipe water to a drinking fountain in the plaza.

He once gave a church in Mexico fifteen hundred dollars for an altar cloth, and he might leave five hundred dollars in any collection plate. In short, he spent money lavishly on everything.

Meanwhile, inevitably, the citizens living on his barony in Arizona were still grumbling. When enough American citizens grumble, they become a political force. It mattered not that Uncle Sam had already eaten humble pie before the baron; these people still hated to see a fancy dandy come in and pre-empt their land. In their minds, legality lost force before moral concepts. The upshot was the creation by Congress of a special Court of Private Land Claims, with the express duty of reviewing Don James's case and all others in dispute.

"By all means let us have such a court," said the baron grandiloquently. "I hear the rumors of discontent. I want my people to be happy. Let this new court review my records. Let certified copies again be brought from the monasteries abroad, showing the line of consanguinity, the true inheritance whereby my wife and I own the barony."

The Spanish government, feeling sympathy for this beleaguered baron in America, went a step farther. To help him, it offered to send not certified copies but the *original* documents themselves. These would be taken from the monastery vaults, sealed, and sent to America under special guard. Then, after official inspection by the new court, they would be returned to their places. Mexico chimed in with a similar offer.

"That's the very thing to do!" Don James agreed again. "Then the matter will be forever settled in all people's minds."

After due diplomatic arrangements, it was done. The original papers, dating back many decades, yellowed with time and written in the quaint idiom of the early Spanish court, were sealed and brought to Arizona. They were locked in a steel vault and placed in the custody of a United States judge and a special marshal. They were, in truth, quite bulky, for economy of words in the old days was not a court consideration in Spain. Every detail of the inheritance was given, even to the complete names of all the ancestors and relatives who might be even remotely involved, plus a physical description of them.

The very first Baron of Arizona—he to whom the Spanish king had originally made the land grant—was named Don Miguel, and his title was a simple "Baron de Arizonac and Caballero de los Colorados, Gentleman of the King's Chamber with privilege to enter at will, Grandee of Spain, Knight of the Military Order of the Golden Fleece and of the Montesa, Knight of the Royal Order of Carlos III, Knight of the Insignia of the Royal College of Our Lady of Guadalupe." He was, the old document further said, "the legitimate son of Don José Gaston Gómez de Silva y Montez de Oca de la Cerda y de Carillo de Peralta de las Falces de la Vega and of Doña Francisca Ana María García de la Córdoba y Muñiz de Perez, who were married in the year 1686."

Thus in detail were all the ancestors described, with the dates of birth, and death, and the marriages of all children right on down to Don James's present wife. The total words in the documents from the monasteries exceeded eighty thousand—more words than one finds in today's average-length novel. But that still wasn't all; by rare good fortune Don James, the present baron, had been able to locate pictures of most of the ancestors—priceless miniatures, and oil paintings—some faded and wrinkled, of course, but good enough to proclaim the obvious aristocracy of the clan. These family portraits were prized in the baron's Arizona home.

Great interest, therefore, attached to the court's display of these documents from Spain and Mexico. Any family which had so distinguished a background and which had established so extraordinary a claim in America was bound to command interest. The court duly convened, the hearing was given in detail, the sealed records from abroad inspected and translated—and once more the baron's claims were substantiated. His barony was all that he said it was. The new court affirmed it. The citizens were flattened once more, without a chance for appeal. *La Baronia de Arizonac* apparently was established in our nation permanently.

Don James, poised and happy, threw a big party to celebrate and began anew to ingratiate himself with the people. He also let contracts for two great sawmills to work his forest land. In conjunction with irrigation, ranching, and mining, he knew that milling would be essential and profitable. He was a builder. He was a great man!

The documents did not go back to Mexico and Spain immediately after court adjourned. They had to wait for the guards to connect with a specific train and boat, and during the interval they were kept in the steel vault at Phoenix. Down at Florence, Arizona, a farm town, lived a quiet-mannered printer named Thomas Weedin. Tom's hobby was study of old type faces, old letters, and old documents of any kind—just a printer's hobby, for recreation and fun. Tom stuttered a little, and that made him unduly shy, but he screwed up nerve enough to go to the United States judge that week.

"J-Judge, your Honor," Tom said humbly, "i-i-if it ain't asking too m-much, I'd sure like to see them old Spanish papers. Just to say I'd s-s-een 'em."

The kindly judge understood. "Why certainly, Tom. I can appreciate your interest in them. They are amusing, for a fact. You go in there to the table in my private office and I'll have the guard bring them out. The guard will have to sit with you, but you won't mind that."

"T-t-thanks."

And so for the next hour Tom Weedin rode his hobby, thumbing old parchments and heavy yellowed papers with holes where leather thongs had been tied in the bindings, with clamps on some, and with all the evidences of age. Here before him were the most important papers in Arizona's history, Tom realized. What a break that he could actually get to handle them. As with most border folk, he spoke enough Spanish to read the documents, and this was joy indeed.

And then—suddenly Tom Weedin stared at a page and grunted.

He blinked and read it again. Hurriedly he turned some more pages and looked back through several he had already read. The more he looked the more excited he became. In another ten minutes he got up abruptly, stammered thanks to the guard, and ran out of the room. The judge was out of his office, but Tom Weedin ran down the street until he found him. He was so excited he could scarcely talk.

"J-J-Judge, your Honor!" he half-whispered. "Them barony p-p-papers, they—they—"

"Yes, Tom? . . . Get hold of yourself!"

"They—they—" Tom pulled the judge's head down and whispered into his ear, and through his excited stuttering came amazing news. The judge's chin dropped; his eyes went wide.

"Sh-h-h, don't say a word about this to anybody else, Tom. Why, that's an astounding thing! Wait till I can take action."

What had you done wrong, Jim? Wherein had the fabric of your daydreams, now woven into reality, become sleazy and thin? We were about to worship you for having done precisely what you wanted to do. Though suspicious, we had seen no reason to suspect you; or else, sinners ourselves, we admired you for having committed the perfect crime. Vicariously we had built with you a castle in the clouds, but at this point ours too is trembling as in an earthquake. The inevitability of righteousness comes with a thunderous roaring.

Months passed, and then one day a federal officer walked up to the magnificent baron, snapped handcuffs on him, and spoke a few crisp words.

"Reavis, the jig's up."

It was up, truly. Tom Weedin, the printer with a hobby of studying old documents, had broken the most amazing case of its kind in American history.

Excitement spread about the territory like a prairie fire when people heard that the baron was arrested. Many were so sold on him by now that they felt he was being framed. About half of the loggers and teamsters who had been sent to his forests quit their jobs and came to town to attend court, ready if necessary to fight with guns for their employer. That was genuine, if mistaken, loyalty.

In United States court at Santa Fé, New Mexico, Uncle Sam challenged the baron with certain facts that the courts had lacked before. What was it that stuttering Tom Weedin, the printer who had a hobby of reading old documents, had whispered in the judge's ear that day?

"T-there's one paper," Tom had said, excitedly, "which is d-d-dated in Madrid, Spain, 1748. But the t-t-type—the type that printed it wasn't invented until 1875!"

"Tom! No!" His Honor was astounded.

"Y-Yes sir! And another one—it-it's dated 1787 in Madrid, but it has a w-w-watermark from a W-Wisconsin paper mill that wasn't even started until after our C-C-Civil War!"

For months, then, federal agents had conducted a new investigation, this time with detailed thoroughness. They went all the way to Mexico City, thence to Madrid itself. Not until they had returned did the judge clamp down on Baron James. At first that worthy was indignant, furious, and threatening. Then he did all that a whipped man could do—broke down and confessed, then pleaded for mercy. His signed confession is available to researchers.

When, some years before, the impecunious Jim Reavis of Missouri chucked his job and disappeared, his name disappeared, too. He wanted no further connection with his mule-driving days, when he was earning barely thirty dollars a month. He had told friends that he yearned to be a Spanish grandee in the Southwest. But he went first to San Francisco, then a boom town, and got himself a job as roving reporter for a newspaper.

With credentials from that paper he "borrowed" money here and there and headed for Mexico, and thence for Spain. Before leaving San Francisco he found an Indian girl, a waif who had been adopted into a white family. She happened to be light-skinned and lovely of face and figure. Jim Reavis stole her from the family, talked to her at length about her ancestry—which he built up in a truly romantic way.

"I have been investigating your past," said he. "You are not Indian at all. You are Spanish. You are the legal heiress of a once-famous California family, and I can prove it."

Of course the girl was interested and excited. Jim entranced her, had a friend perform a fake marriage ceremony, and took his "bride" to Mexico.

They lived a gay life for a while, then Jim began to lay the most incredible groundwork for fraud in history. In the streets of Mexico, and later in Spain he learned the Spanish language well. He delved into ancient libraries, studying the idiom of forgotten days. He probed old curio shops and bought miniatures and oil paintings (some of them well done) of people who he claimed were his wife's ancestors. The girl, no conspirator in his fraud, believed literally everything he told her.

"This is your great-great-grandmother," he would say, of one picture which he had found. "She has your eyes, Sofia."

In Mexico and in Spain he hired street scribes to whom he dictated long, leisurely documents to be written or printed on the heaviest paper he could buy. He would leave the paper in the hot sun in order to give it the appearance of age. When it was ready, he would take it to the monasteries where legal documents had been stored for centuries.

"I am an American newspaper writer," he told the monks. "Could I do some research in your ancient records, in order to write a book about Spain?"

Of course he could. He had credentials, which were faked, and a personal charm which was ingratiating. The monks, happy to accommodate an American journalist, opened old, creaky doors and showed him the musty tomes of yesteryear. Then they would leave him alone with lantern or candles for hours at a time.

When they left, he would turn to the proper dates in a box or volume of court records, tear out the genuine documents, and insert the papers he had cleverly forged.

One day a monk hovered near him, visiting and offering to be of service. Jim Reavis couldn't get rid of him and suddenly fell over in a "faint."

"*Por Dios!*" the frightened monk exclaimed. "The foul air in this vault has sickened him. I must go for help!"

This was exactly what Jim had planned. When the monk ran away, Jim jumped up, made his substitution as before, stuffed the discarded old papers into his boot tops, and lay down "unconscious" again. The monk and two helpers came back and revived him with wine and water, then carried him out into the fresh air. Jim was very grateful.

In such a manner Jim Reavis altered the sacred records of two nations, to confound the monks and the first investigators who were sent to trail him.

At the trial Mrs. Reavis—whom Jim had called Doña Sofia Loreto—took the witness stand. "We were never really

married, I realize now," said she. "And I'm sure I really am
an Indian, not a Spaniard. But I believed him until you
brought me here. He was very kind to me. I loved him, and
he loved me. I don't know what to do."

When his ultimate conviction was assured, she divorced
him (an unnecessary action) and proudly began to earn a
living for herself and her twin sons. The last record we have
of them states that she was working as a chambermaid in a
hotel—she who had once "owned" twelve million acres and
been entertained at an ambassador's ball.

But what of Don James? Strange indeed are the vagaries
of American nature. For perpetrating the greatest fraud on
record, Jim Reavis perhaps should have been hanged or given
a life sentence. But good or bad, he was a charming man. He
had a strong political following and many personal friends.
The jury sentenced him to prison for only six years! What
is more, pressure continued to be brought to bear in his behalf, and he served but two years of the sentence.

For years afterward he remained a prominent figure in
the Southwest. He was seen in Phoenix in 1910, still talking
and writing freely about his "Andalusian beauty, Doña
Sofia Loreto." He wrote of her: "Her features were exquisite.
Her eyes were large, and of darkest hazel. A profusion of
black and silken hair hung to her waist when I married her.
The delicate lines of her body, and her exquisite grace and
fascination, told of noble ancestry. She was of splendid
physique, elastic step, and a superb dancer."

Photographs of her tend in some measure to bear him
out. In one such, showing her dressed in her Spanish finery,
she is lovely, indeed. Another, taken years later beside the
rock which marked the western boundary line of the
"barony," shows her to be too heavy. The former Don
James liked to talk of her to anyone who would listen.

In Phoenix, after his prison days, Reavis tried to promote

several enterprises. He wanted to establish three large lumber mills in central Arizona and said he could raise the money for it. He also wanted to dig an irrigation canal from the Colorado River to Central Arizona—a "fantastic" enterprise which, thirty years later, was considered entirely feasible. He tried writing, lecturing, and ranching for a living. None of these efforts succeeded. For a time people helped him with loans of money, which he dissipated on fruitless schemes of a minor nature.

Finally he disappeared once more. There is some evidence to show when and where he died, but this has not been fully substantiated. Probably he would like to be remembered as a mystery man anyway, so imaginative was his nature.

By way of epitaph we can quote a statement by William M. Tipton, the government agent who headed the investigation that finally exposed Don James. Said Tipton, "No plan of fraud was ever more ingeniously devised, none ever carried out with greater patience, industry, and skill."

Mr. Tipton made that statement in 1896, and it still holds.

7

JUDGE ROY BEAN, THE GREAT LOVER

ONE COULD never claim appreciable knowledge of the South-west without being acquainted with an impossible old son of Satan named Roy Bean. The newcomer may not believe half he hears about him, but in time he will learn that the yarns about Roy Bean fade in color when set beside the documented facts. He was undoubtedly the damndest gent ever to operate on the vast sunlit stage known as Texas—which is saying a great deal. I hasten to add that he does not typify native Texans; for they are God's Chosen People, and all of them go to heaven when they die. Roy was an immigrant foreigner from Kentucky or somewhere in that vicinity, and in their compassion the Texans let him stay because he had fought on their side in the late unpleasantness with the Yankees. Well-known authors have devoted entire books to this worthy individual; after this brief presentation the reader can pursue his career in detail.

I like to introduce Roy Bean via Lew Hubbard, which is, I believe, a fictional name. Lew made a fatal mistake one day in the eighteen nineties for which he really should not be blamed. He just hadn't reckoned with the ardor of that great lover and public servant, Roy Bean. The trouble did not stem from the fact that the framed picture of Lily Lang-try caught Lew's eye as he turned to put his whisky glass down on Roy Bean's bar. The trouble started when Lew, in a moment of poor judgment, said, "Ah-h-h! There's a heifer worthy of any man's corral!" Nor was the statement particularly unfortunate, except for the fact that Roy Bean, polishing glasses behind the bar, was within earshot. And, quicker than it takes to tell it, Roy had plugged Lew with lead from each of his two pistols.

Six or eight men witnessed the shooting, but none dared to move or speak. Still holding his guns, Mr. Bean addressed them. "As coroner of this district," said he, "I appoint you men on a jury. That there, men, is a dead corpse. What is yore verdict as to how come him to die?"

Two or three of them swallowed, somewhat audibly, but it was Bart Gobble, Roy's right-hand man, who first regained his tongue.

"Why—why, Judge, Yore Honor—it seems like a open and shut case of—of—suicide. That's it—suicide! That's our verdict—ain't it, men?"

The others nodded hasty agreement, and Roy Bean holstered his guns.

That episode was characteristic of Roy Bean. Folks down on the Llano Estacado of Texas still speak of him as if he might come riding up over the horizon at any moment; they'll still be talking about him a hundred years from now.

What manner of person was this, who could deliberately shoot a man and have it called suicide? Why should he have taken offense at a leering jest about an actress performing two thousand miles away?

Mr. Bean was an opportunist who did a spell of mule whacking and fought Indians in Texas. One day he learned that a railroad was planning to push its main line westward from San Antonio to El Paso.

"Why, darn it, there's a ten-day stretch out there with only one good water hole!" Roy suddenly remembered.

Forthwith, he loaded a wagon with whisky, lumber, and

flour and started out. He knew positively that the railroad must be routed near that source of precious water, which lay west of the Pecos River—normally too alkaline to drink —out in the Texas arid lands. Civilization hadn't penetrated there, other than what fleeing criminals and occasional travelers had brought into the territory. When the railroad crews and their inevitable followers arrived, Roy Bean was owner *in toto* of the water supply. He wore two young cannons and stood ready to enforce his claim with them. He had erected a cabin, in which he operated a store and a saloon. He advertised beer at a dollar a bottle, a price thirsty newcomers were happy to pay.

Mr. Bean announced that this was a town and that he had named it Vinegaroon, Texas, because of large numbers of vinegaroon scorpions found near by. Moreover, he said he was mayor, postmaster, coroner, owner, justice of the peace, and judge. And did any one care to dispute it?

One half of his cabin was given over to a whisky bar. The other was used as the court, where Judge Bean meted out a dubious justice. By the simple process of removing his theoretically white apron, the bartender was metamorphosed into a judge. This he began to do at increasingly frequent intervals as the population of the region increased.

Horse thieving was then the major crime in the Southwest. And a horse thief, brought in by ranchers from some distance away, was the first to question the jurisdiction of His Honor, Judge Roy Bean.

"So you figger I ain't got no jurisdiction to try ye, eh?" Judge Bean eyed the criminal. "Waal, Bart, where are ye?"

Bart Gobble, his man Friday and a physical giant, stepped out.

"Bart, ef I say take this horse thief out and string him up, what'll ye do, eh?"

"Why Judge, Yore Honor, I'll jest nacherlly hang him, accordin' to law."

106

"Waal, that's my ruling', by gobs! Take the prisoner out and show him my jurisdiction, Bart."

Fifteen minutes later, the prisoner was dangling by his neck outside, where Bart Gobble, singlehanded, had stretched him.

No lawyers practiced in Judge Bean's court, because there were none closer than San Antonio or maybe Fort Worth—a long journey to the east. Once, however, a west Texan with money, who got into trouble with Judge Bean's handmade law, appeared before His Honor. He begged for time and got it. When he next appeared there, he was represented by a genuine attorney, an astute gentleman from a distant town.

The lawyer, having done some research, made it plain that he was out of patience with the whole peremptory business and that he was there to see justice done.

"My investigation reveals, Bean, that you are neither a justice nor a judge; that you have presumed to all such authority as you exercise; that you have no right whatsoever to hold my client under bond or otherwise; and that you are in fact yourself guilty of malfeasance and felonious misrepresentation." The attorney made quite a speech of it, and somewhat in that manner, according to the recollection of witnesses.

His Honor—His Self-appointed Honor—expectorated a generous quantity of tobacco juice across the judicial table before he spoke.

"Bart!" he barked. "Where are ye?"

"Right here at hand, Yore Honor," the giant replied.

"Ef I say to string up this prisoner, what'll ye do, Bart?"

"Why, I'll string him, Yore Honor."

"Ef I say to string up this two-bit lawyer along with him, what'll ye do?"

"'Tain't no trouble to hang two at once, Yore Honor."

Judge Bean eyed the lawyer significantly. Precedent—on which the great bulk of all law rests—was notoriously against the attorney and his client. The hostility of the crowd was almost tangible. Bart Gobble had, indeed, hanged two men at once on other occasions, although sometimes it had been necessary for him to shoot one first. Judge Bean waited impatiently. It was only a matter of seconds until the counselor resigned his job and departed toward Dallas.

Judge Bean had somehow acquired a few of the physical accouterments of a courtroom, including a notarial seal, a gavel, and an old book. (The book listed some of the early Texas laws but was quite useless after the Civil War.) He learned, too, that officers could have deputies, and when business boomed he was assisted by the late W. H. Dodd.

With these props, Roy Bean would sit at his rough, home-made table and conduct court. If the weather was warm, he would shove the table out on the front porch and sit on a beer keg while frontier justice was dispensed. The "jail" was right at hand—a great log with chains attached, ready for clamping around criminals' ankles. Sometimes a minor offender would get a term of several days "in jail," and on long summer evenings His Honor and the available loafers would play cards with the prisoner or just sit and swap yarns. (The Judge especially liked to talk about Lily Langtry—but respectfully, always.) The Court saw no reason why sociability should be ruled out just because punishment was ruled in.

Judge Bean could read and write only with difficulty, but at each trial he would pretend to search his one book of antiquated law. When he "found" the statutes for each particular case, he announced his findings with profundity. Punishment usually was one of three things—death by hanging, a term in jail, or a stiff fine. Sometimes all three were combined, and invariably the property of executed men was confiscated. His Honor's favorite exclamation was "By gobs!", which, together with the statement "That's my rulin'," closed every court verdict. Moreover, after sentence had been pronounced, there was no long legal shilly-shallying; Deputy Bart Gobble carried out the punishment at once.

Deputy Dodd kept so-called records, but there is no dependable account of the number of prisoners ordered hanged by Judge Bean, or of the other cases over which he presided. His position as coroner provided Bean with a remunerative side line. That expanse of west Texas attracted a great many fugitives—human derelicts of all kinds, who seemed, eventually, to get killed.

Coroner Bean never went out to view a body. The body was always thrown across a horse, or in a hack, and brought to him. It would be dumped there in the front yard, and presently the coroner would leave his whisky bar and come out for the official hearing. This usually entailed sitting directly on the corpse itself, while the late lamented's pockets were searched and contents confiscated. "What'd he do to git hisself shot?" Judge Bean would inquire.

"Tried to steal a man's saddle, suh," replied a citizen on one occasion.

"Stealin', eh! Waal, for that I fine him ten dollars. But he ain't got only five dollars in his pockets, so I'll hold this gun o' his as security for the rest."

It must be understood that none of this was in any way humorous to the participants. It was a serious, effective procedure, although irregular as we view official machinery today. There was simply no one to challenge Roy Bean effectively, no one with strength or interest enough to call his gigantic bluff and make him back down.

Of course, his reputation spread. When the state officials at faraway Austin heard of him, they wrote him for an accounting of the fees he'd collected. They were willing to let him preside, it appeared, inasmuch as he was doing a fair job of it, if he would check in at headquarters with occasional reports.

"Don't worry none about me," he wrote back. "I aim to make my court self-supporting."

But he did more than that. By heavy fines, by confiscations, and by marriage, divorce, christening, and burial fees, he made his court positively prosperous. And he had the additional income from the sale of liquor and assorted merchandise.

As the years passed and Val Verde County was organized, news got around that it was official election time in the great state of Texas. An election was all right with Roy Bean; he never was one to oppose the people's will. He would run for all of the offices he held, which he did—and woe to any candidate who dared oppose him! One man, of Mexican blood, who decided to be a candidate, was soon found mysteriously dead. When Coroner Bean investigated, it was ruled that the man died of gross carelessness, which, in a sense, was true. After his first unanimous election, Mr. Bean just didn't bother to campaign in the future, and since nobody seemed interested in having his authority officially renewed, he just went on presiding. Often people shot at him, and a few lived—for a while—thereafter. Roy Bean was active and deadly with guns. He made mysterious night sallies. He didn't have many enemies—that is, none who could admit their enmity for long.

You will recall that Lew Hubbard met his Waterloo because of his remark about Lily Langtry's picture over Roy Bean's whisky bar. You see, the day Roy, acting as postmaster, clipped Lily's picture from a magazine, he fell desperately in love. That was early in his career at Vinegaroon.

Lovely Lily was the toast of Manhattan then. Moreover,

she was internationally famous. She was so sought after in London that she could—and did—drop ice down the back of the Prince of Wales. The Prince's dignity reputedly suffered, but Lily's fame mounted still more.

In New York, hundreds of men paid court to her, but she accepted none. Lily Langtry—"The Jersey Lily" they called her—was a headliner in the best shows, the criterion of all beauty as the century drew to a close. Her fame penetrated even to distant, frontier Vinegaroon.

Roy Bean had never married. Perhaps he had never thought of it—at least not until he clipped Lily's picture. When he put it in a frame over his whisky bar, he enshrined it in his heart as well.

Bean had had sundry signs painted over his cabin:

JUDGE ROY BEAN
NOTARY PUBLIC ·
JUSTICE OF THE PEACE
Ice Beer
Billiard Hall
LAW WEST OF THE PECOS

"Law West of the Pecos"! He was literally that, the only champion of law in a vast, wild territory. Presumptuous, cruel, unrelenting, he nevertheless did a great deal of good. He cleaned out many genuine rascals, and the better element of society not only tolerated him but encouraged him in his astounding career. Most of the citizens were uninterested in the technical point of jurisdiction anyway; results alone counted. To his array of shingles, Roy Bean now had another sign added. This new sign gave the saloon its official name:

THE JERSEY LILLY

The name was to honor Lily Langtry, and her alone. Nobody apparently noticed or cared about the extra *l*. Postmaster Bean clipped more pictures and nailed them up. He began to talk of her incessantly. He almost worshiped her, it seemed. Moreover, he began to write her a letter every day.

Soon he informed the President and the Postmaster General of the United States that the post office and town of Vinegaroon, Texas, was henceforth and thereafter to be honored with a new name. Vinegaroon became *Langtry*, Texas, by gobs! And official Washington accepted the change as commanded. Incidentally, to this day a map of west Texas shows the town of Langtry, where the Jersey Lilly cabin, signs and all, may still be seen.

The daily love letters to Lily Langtry were an outlet for Roy's emotions, even though they never elicited a reply. Lily probably got dozens of love letters every week, but

Roy Bean didn't think of that. An uneducated, unrefined man, he labored hard over his letters. It is a shame that none of them has been preserved. It is amazing what an influence the actress, whose acquaintance he never made, had on the fierce but lonely frontier man.

One day a young cowpuncher was haled into Judge Bean's court and duly tried. The trial was simply a matter of taking ten minutes' testimony, wherein it was learned that two witnesses had seen the accused steal a horse. As sure as the devil made rattlesnakes, the boy would have been hanged within another hour, so strict was the range law.

As usual, however, Judge Bean adjourned court for a brief recess before pronouncing sentence. The Judge crossed over behind the liquor bar, with witnesses, deputies, and spectators in front. If any person ever declined to order a drink under such circumstances, it usually was construed as contempt of court, with a resultant fine.

On this particular day, the hapless prisoner, drinking his last whisky, chanced to see the Judge's beloved picture.

"Ain't that there Miss Lily Langtry?" the boy suddenly asked. "Why, I ain't seen her since we was back East that time!"

The boy seemed honest about it, and probably was. Judge Bean stared at him. "You say you seen her, *yoreself?*" His Honor demanded.

"Yes, sir, I did. She was wonderful, she was. Never have I seen a lady as beautiful and as fine as she was. Reminded me of my own mother, when she was young. Only Miss Lily was even prettier."

The court recess was automatically extended nearly an hour. Judge Bean plied the youngster with questions. They had a heart-to-heart talk about La Belle Langtry, including all the details of her stage performances and frequent and respectful references to her beauty.

When court finally was called to order again, the Judge's sentence was swift and sure:

"Nobody responsible seen you take that horse, son. I'm tired of havin' innocent men brought in here, by gobs! Bart, fine the men that brought this boy in here ten dollars apiece for contempt of court. Prisoner discharged, and that's my rulin'."

Lover Bean must have written several hundred letters to Lily Langtry before he decided to take further action in his romance. Then one day he suddenly announced that he had to go to San Antonio on business. He delegated all his powers to deputies, took a pocketful of money and his two pistols, and headed east.

He went much farther than San Antonio, though. He went to the town where Lily Langtry was currently playing and bought a seat in the front row of the theater.

The next night he bought another seat, and the next. Lily had lived up to expectations, and more. If he had been in love with her picture, he was even more so with Lily in person. As she moved from town to town, he followed. He saw her as often as he could—from a distance. He never spoke to her, never made an effort to meet her directly, even though he had traveled thousands of miles. He was content to feast his eyes from an orchestra seat. Perhaps he sensed that he was, after all, an uncouth frontiersman with blood on his record and no whit of polish, even on the surface. Lily never saw him. In due time his money ran out, and he came on back home to resume his letter-writing.

By rights, some stronger, quicker, braver man should ultimately have turned up in Langtry, Texas, to challenge Roy Bean and kill him in a dramatic gun-shooting showdown. Or some relative of an executed prisoner, some brother of a Mexican horse thief, or some envious gambler should have knifed Roy Bean in the back or shot him from ambush.

But the "Law West of the Pecos" wasn't destined to pass out that way. On the morning of March 16, 1903, he died peacefully in his bunk.

Nobody wept, yet his funeral attracted widespread attention. A few men with a sense of fitness did erect a simple marker, which still stands. Its inscription merely says, "Judge Roy Bean, Justice of the Peace, Law West of the Pecos." It was enough. It marked the end of a chapter, in the history of the West. Not many people knew or cared about Roy's personal romance. Philosophers have told us that life has but one tragedy—unrequited love; but people had scant time for philosophy in the Río Grande country then, and even now simple existence is still a he-man occupation in that great expanse of land.

There is, however, a denouement to Roy Bean's beautiful love story.

One day a fast through train made an unscheduled stop at the station of Langtry, Texas. From a special car at the end a lovely lady stepped down. She asked the station agent a question.

"Why, ma'am, he's been dead these two months now!" the gaping agent told her.

"It's a shame," the beautiful lady said sincerely. "I did so want to meet him, and thank him for all the sweet love letters, and have him show me the town he named for me."

8

CLOVER IN THE COFFIN

TEX AKERS was squatting by the frying pan and leaning back comically to dodge smoke from the breakfast fire, when he saw his partner running back up the slope toward him. Something in the other man's manner caused Tex to set the pan of bacon aside, pick up a rifle, and walk out a way.

"What is it, Trav?" he demanded of Travis White.

"Forty, fifty head. Come on."

They had camped on a bluff above the Pecos River in Texas. The dawn was still gray.

"Our'n?" Tex asked, as they walked fast.

"I couldn't see no brand. But they look mighty like Dollbaby stuff. All young stock."

He meant that intuition had told him something that his eyes couldn't see. The cattle, or the calves at any rate, would be from the Dollbaby ranch but would be maverick stuff driven out of the brush that lined the river. It would look familiar because any good cowboy gets to know his cattle almost as individuals. And yet—

"It wouldn't do to make too many mistakes," Tex warned.

These same two had already been in one shooting scrape with some men they thought were rustlers and had killed a Mexican and a stranger from back East. It had subsequently been shown that the victims were innocent. But Judge Roy

Bean, who presided at Tex's and Trav's trial had said that the killings were honest mistakes and that nobody but a fool would be acting like rustlers, no matter how innocent. So Tex and Travis had gone free.

Now they were scouting again. Old Man White, Travis' father, had estimated that a good third of his calf crop had been stolen this season, but he needed proof about who had done the stealing. This was in the heyday of cattle rustling along the Big Bend of the Río Grande, back in the eighteen eighties.

"Only thing is," Travis warned now, "it's six or eight men driving them calves, and we're only two."

"You afraid?" Tex Akers scoffed.

"Hell, no!"

"Well, then."

They had to run-walk nearly a mile before they could see the moving stock and the riders behind them, but by angling south another mile they saw a chance to intercept the herd as it passed a dry lake bed. There wouldn't be much cover for ambush, although the gray dawn would help them get there unseen, Tex pointed out.

They made it, by crawling the last hundred yards. Snakeweed and other brush served to hide them, if not to protect them from possible bullets. Akers moved fifty yards away from his pal, saying he would shoot first as a signal. In a very few minutes a cloud of alkali dust, stirred up by the cattle, was floating before them, and the petulant "Bawr-r-r" of the yearlings could be heard. The riders, all too dark and bearded to be recognized at the two-hundred-yard range, were "talking" to their charges, "Hyah-hyah, git! Huy-huy!" and urging them on as fast as possible without actually running them. From behind his clump of brush, Tex Akers strained to see some sort of brand. He hoped to see the simple outline of a doll—head, body, arms, and legs—

which was the brand mark of Old Man White's ranch, but he couldn't see a single one. And yet, as Travis White had said, he too sensed that these were White animals now streaming before him.

"Hell," mumbled Akers, taking aim—and taking a chance.

Crack! His rifle bruised his shoulder, but he fired again and again. Out there in the alkali and gray light, one man slumped over in his saddle and screamed in pain.

Travis White was shooting too, now, but there was a grand stir among the riders. They and the cattle seemed to catch the alarm simultaneously, and all fled in fear. The riders shot back but saw no targets. They had no way of guessing how many persons were attacking them, and they didn't wait to find out. They lay low in their saddles—those who were able—and disappeared to the southeast, while the cattle stampeded in every direction.

Half an hour later, Akers and White found one man stone dead and saw his riderless horse in the distance.

"I think we got another'n," Akers said. "But he made it off."

They turned over the body of the dead man. Neither knew who he was—just one of a thousand nondescript strangers who had drifted into this West-of-the-Pecos region in the past year or two. There was no proof yet that he was a rustler.

He was left there for the buzzards to pick, a symbol of the casual attitude toward death in west Texas in that era, and the two cowboys returned to their unfinished breakfast. After eating they rode to the Dollbaby lands and found all the proof they needed. Not only were there tracks, but a dozen or more cows with Dollbaby brands were lowing heads extended and eyes wild, seeking their calves.

"They didn't take nothing but unbranded stock," Akers said, cursing. "They couldn't be trapped in no court."

There wasn't any court, save the impromptu ones of ranchers and the self-appointed judiciary of Justice Roy Bean. And yet the better ranchers of the region clung to Bean's precedent, rank though his decisions sometimes were.

"But they were rustlers," Travis White said. "I'm glad we got at least one."

They went back to the ranch headquarters. Akers took some men to round up the stampeded stock, while Travis White rode in to the town of Vinegaroon, where Judge Bean presided, to report what had occurred. The judge was quietly indignant. He was no saint himself, but he resented any lawlessness in his territory as a personal affront.

"I'll just take and sashay around the country some," he said to White. "You wanta come along?"

They rode all day, Bean's corpulent body bouncing jelly-like on a slow horse. White didn't enjoy the trip, because it seemed to be pointless. Bean, for instance, led him up to the distant ranch house of one Ike Smith and stopped, apparently to make a social call.

"Don't see no sign of nobody home," the Judge said, after calling loudly and then rapping on the front door. "Let's set a while anyhow, son."

They sat on the small front porch for nearly an hour, talking idly about weather and screwworms and dehorning Texas longhorns and such allied topics as interested cattlemen. But Ike Smith didn't show up, and the two men finally rode on.

They called at the McGuire ranch, about six miles farther, and elected to spend the night there and return to Vinegaroon the next day. Mr. McGuire was at home. Also, by chance, Alec Dubose of the Yes Jenny outfit was there. Judge Bean was happy to see both men, and young White was friendly with them.

"I been out scouting for some of my stock that's lost," Dubose mentioned, while they waited for supper.

"That a fact?" the Judge encouraged.

"Judge, I tell you my Y-J ain't been burned on half as many calves this year as it was last. And I got nearly twice as many breed cows and heifers. I cain't believe the coyotes gits that many."

"Human coyotes," Travis White put in, bitterly.

"If I only knowed who."

"You men're hintin' it's up to me as judge," Bean nodded. "Well I'm doin' what I can. Right now I say I'll offer a thousand-dollar reward for anybody'll kill or collect them rustlers. They been raidin' a dozen places or more."

"I'll match that with another thousand," Mr. Dubose said.

"Me too," said McGuire.

Travis White spoke up respectfully. "I bet papa will match you men. If he won't, I will. I own a little stock myself."

"This reward becomes talkin' money, then," the Judge said. He meant that it was an impressive sum, enough to spur somebody to action. And right away Dubose himself spoke up.

"Four thousand dollars is more than I cleared all last year. Be damned if I don't go rustler hunting myself."

"I could go with you," Travis White offered.

They made a deal of it. The Dollbaby and Yes Jenny ranches had suffered heavy losses for more than three years, which was exasperating as well as costly. White got permission from his father to live on the Yes Jenny and, on the quiet, do some work with Alec Dubose as a range detective. Judge Bean promised to back their play if and when a showdown came.

Dubose was probably one of the shrewdest ranchers ever to herd cattle in Texas, as well as one of the gentlest. Not in the least tough or quick to anger, he was a true gentleman. His Y-J brand, for instance, was dubbed the Yes Jenny because of his devotion to his wife. Some even said he was henpecked, and he'd just grin and admit it. His Y-J—really the Y-J Connected—commanded respect everywhere, but nobody would have thought of the man himself as being an officer or a person clever at tracking down rustlers.

"That's the very reason I encouraged him," Judge Bean told a few solid citizens confidentially. "He ain't the type, and so he won't be suspected. Jest Yes-Jenny Dubose and the kid Travis White—who'd think they were out hunting outlaws?"

The first thing the two did was ride far off and scout the country toward Mexico. People had said that the stolen cattle might have been taken over the border. But the two detectives could find no evidence of it. Some of the Mexican families in Texas, devout Catholic folk more honest than prosperous, had lived and worked along there for years, and they had seen no evidence of cattle stealing.

"What say we drift on up to El Paso, son?" Dubose suggested then to Travis White.

"We couldn't get any rustlers cornered there, could we?"

"Never can tell."

So they went to the famed border town and called on several well-known bankers and cattle buyers. Mr. Dubose would work the conversation around to the subject on his mind.

"Who all's been shipping heaviest lately from down our way?" he would ask.

One buyer, a Chicagoan, said, "Well, the old timers are about on the same level, but some of the newer men are coming up. There's a fellow in Presidio been increasing his sales mighty fast. Another, named Locksley, had some mighty fat steers and plenty of 'em, from the Lenox Flats area. And— lemme see, ain't Ike Smith somewheres close to your ranches, men? He runs the Clover Leaf brand? Well, he oughta be sporting a good bank account, he's been shoving some fine young stock through every year lately."

That's the way the talk went. Dubose collected about a dozen names in the little black tally book he always carried in his inside coat pocket. He didn't explain much to young White because, he said, he never liked to talk unless he was sure what he was talking about.

"What'll we do now?" White asked.

"Go home. And ride hossback again."

They had traveled to a village some fifty miles from the Yes Jenny ranch when Mr. Dubose suddenly recognized a Mexican woman who was walking toward them.

"Candelaria," he greeted her, "what are you doing away up here? You're nearly a hundred miles from home."

"*Señor, mi amigo.*" She was very respectful. "I coom on the burro. The weather she is not hot now."

"October, yeah. But you rode burro-back one hundred miles for what?"

"They tell me you would stop here, *señor*. My hosban' he must work, so I coom. Is the cattles. *Las vacas, amigo.* Is the many of them the young ones, *sí*. Is the water and the fire and the men who wear the black hairs and frighten our daughters and they have—"

"Candelaria! Speak Mexican, so I can understand you. If you are trying to say what I think you are—!"

She was truly excited. Now speaking in her own tongue, she made herself clear. Both Dubose and White could understand her, and when they had given her some money and profuse thanks, they hastened to the village store.

"I want a case of ammunition," Dubose ordered. "Forty-fives, and some rifle stuff. Say about—"

They loaded it in their buggy and started traveling faster. Dubose opined that a Mexican friend is truly a loyal one, and White concurred. When they reached home, they quietly selected five trusted cowboys, armed them heavily, and took provisions for a two weeks' trip.

"Where you folks going?" a chance visitor at the ranch said.

"Deer hunting," Dubose lied. "Up north. Been promising these boys a big vacation hunt. Now we aim to take it. Plumb into New Mexico, I reckon. Up Ruidoso way."

He hoped that would pass for the truth, but when he saw the glint in the eyes of his men, he had serious doubts. There was no gaiety, no hilarity, such as would have accompanied preparations for a deer hunt. Instead there was a deadly seriousness in the demeanor of these cowboys.

What the chance visitor did about it—if anything—nobody will ever know. History has even lost his name now. But he left the Y-J ranch immediately after the cowboys did. They rode north as promised, but he struck out toward the south and was never seen again.

After riding scarcely five miles northward, the five cowboys traveling with Dubose and White, armed as if for battle, began to circle. They made a long three-day ride and expended most of their horses' energies not by sun but by starlight.

"Least anybody sees us, the better we'll be," Dubose ruled.

On the fourth day, as the Mexican woman Candelaria had told them, they came to a watering place far to the southwest of the Yes Jenny and Dollbaby ranches, far out of Judge Bean's normal jurisdiction. And sure enough, there in a kind of vast natural corral formed by low cliffs and canyons which surrounded a water hole and good grass, were some two thousand yearlings. Dubose and his men scouted them one dawn.

"We cain't afford to make no mistakes," Dubose ruled. "Now let's string out about a rod or two apart and creep up close. If we still can't see what's what, I'll go on alone and see if I can identify any of them animals."

"It ain't nary a man in sight," young Travis White worried.

"May be a guard way down the slope, where the canyon opens. If they are rustlers, they'd be off getting more stuff to bring here. You can see where branding fires have been. And a camp site over there by them trees."

The absence of anyone working or guarding so fine a herd still worried White, but he suffered Mr. Dubose to go out alone to reconnoiter. Dubose was about two hundred yards ahead of the other six men, who kept low in the grass.

Their horses had been tied in brush nearly a mile back, but each man carried sidearms and a rifle in his hand, although there was nothing visible which might require use of them.

Dubose came back in half an hour to report. "Every one of them animals has some kind of brand on it, near as I can see. I couldn't fully make out what, but they're branded."

"That makes it bad," White said.

"Yep. Only thing we can do is slip back, get our horses, and ride up bold like, to see what we can see. We can state that we are looking for a stampeded herd of mares."

Their discussion, however, ended on a tragic note. From some invisible point a rifle spoke.

Travis White groaned, swung around. His rifle fell from his hands. The other men, including Dubose, gazed stupidly at him for a second or two, transfixed by sheer surprise. But then—

"My God, he's been shot!" somebody said.

Instantly everybody dropped to the ground. And in the same instant—almost on the echo of the first shot—more rifles were fired.

"Scatter, and fight like hell!" Dubose ordered, quite unnecessarily.

White had died immediately. The next volley wounded a chap named Ferron, who subsequently died. And in the ensuing few minutes bullets flew so fast both ways that Dubose was hit twice and two more of his men were badly hurt.

Dubose was cursing, but he saw that at least a dozen rifles were trained on them from three sides. He and his cowboys had almost no cover or breastworks.

"Somebody trapped us," he ground out. "They'll kill us all in ten minutes more. I'll see if I can get a parley."

He had no white handkerchief, but he raised his big hat and waved it. The firing stopped.

Somebody shouted derisively, "Stand up! Drop your guns!"

They had no choice but to obey. Those who could stood up.

Presently, fourteen armed men had surrounded them, and their leader came a few steps forward.

"All right, you low-down rustlers!" he called. "Did you think you could raid this herd right before our eyes?"

"Why—! That's Smith!" Dubose breathed. "Ike Smith! And he says *we're* rustlers!"

It took a lot of talking to square things.

Ike Smith, of the Clover Brand sure enough, was boss here. He had come this far south to buy young stock, brand it, hold it until he had a sizable herd, then drive it to his home range. The men with him testified that this was true. Dubose knew none of them, and they all looked like outlaws, but he had to take Smith at his word. Besides—Dubose and his own men might well be hanged here, for attempted rustling!

"Only reason I believe you, Dubose," Smith said, "is that you ain't on your hosses. I reckon you might've been just snooping to see if this was stolen stock. So git out. Git out with yore dead and yore wounded, before we do string you all up."

Dubose got out with what was left of his party and carried out the dead. He himself had to be heavily bandaged. He had lost a lot of blood and might easily have died. The procession reached the home ranch in due time, sadly bedraggled in body and spirits; they had gone out after rustlers and failed.

When they finally reported to Judge Bean, that worthy was indignant because of the Mexican woman's false tip. Dubose insisted that it wasn't necessarily false, that he had known her for years and trusted her. And yet—

"All the cattle we got close to there," he confessed, "had Smith's Three-leaf Clover brand on 'em. That's legal ownership. And if we go off half-cocked, trying to prove some dirt about those brands, we can get into all sorts of legal and moral trouble."

It was true. A brand was almost sacred, a positive seal of ownership on any animal. The men gave some thought to the way in which Smith's band had hidden out and ambushed them. Could the stranger who left Dubose's home that day have been a spy? Some thought yes, but it was mere guesswork, so far.

All in all, there was no whit of evidence to prove that Ike Smith was guilty, and when Ike himself began to say that he was a cattle buyer and a breeder, people had to let it go at that. On the other hand, as Alec Dubose kept saying to his close friends, there wasn't anybody around selling cattle to Smith, nor was there any news of Smith's making long drives from distant places. There were no accurate range statistics in those days. Every man just made an estimate of his stock. People said the government ought to keep closer tab on things, but this step wasn't to come for decades yet.

"Keep trying," Judge Bean urged. "You'll pick up a clue yet."

Dubose and two of his cowboys, trusted friends named Cliff Karpe and Pete Ragley, quietly spent about six months counting cattle. They rode far and wide, counting their own, their neighbors', and those on any ranches fringing theirs for many miles around. They kept records in their tally books of all the cows, bulls, and steers under each brand, until they were satisfied that they had a fairly accurate census.

Ike Smith turned out to have 2,221 cows or heifers of breeding age and scarcely 500 market steers that season. But at the next big drive to market less than a year after the count, Smith sold nearly 800 steers.

"His cows couldn't have give birth to grown-up animals that way," Cliff Karpe remarked saltily.

"He's convicted himself," Pete Ragley agreed. "Let's move in on him, boss."

"You men come with me," Dubose ordered. "And keep quiet."

A month later he led them one day to the far corner of his own lands, nearly ten miles from home, crossed the unfenced boundary between his and Smith's property, and deliberately dropped a lariat rope on a young Clover Leaf steer. They downed the animal, then dismounted to inspect it.

"That's a good clean brand, all right," Dubose said. "It's a clover leaf plain as day. And not over two months old. Smith's brand."

"It ain't likely he'd let this steer get grown before branding," Karpe suggested.

"He could have, though. Might not have been caught in the roundup. But all right, men, I know what you're wanting. Shoot the critter, and let's skin it back."

Pete Ragley pulled his gun and shot the steer. Karpe already had out a long sharp pocket knife, and Dubose opened his, too. In scarcely five minutes they had cut the steer's tough hide and carefully laid back an area on the left side.

"Hah!" Karpe suddenly exclaimed.

Dubose began muttering curses. Ragley spat in anger. They stood up, wiping blood off their knives and staring at the evidence before them.

"Let's ride, gents," Dubose said. "It's too long a ways to Vinegaroon. And if Judge Bean wants to see for himself, we can bring him here later."

"What's yore plan, boss?" Karpe asked.

"You're the best roper here," Dubose said. "Now you

lag behind us when we git close to his house. And then. . . ."

They planned their action with care. It was six miles to the Clover Leaf headquarters and to the house where Ike Smith lived alone. He had no wife or family and seldom had anybody living with him. His cowboys usually worked from field cabins, miles away.

"If he ain't there, we'll wait," Dubose said. "This thing has come to a head."

But Ike Smith, as luck would have it, was at home. It was around 5:00 P.M. when Dubose and Pete Ragley rode into sight, down the slope near Smith's front porch. Smith came out, rifle in hand.

"That you, Dubose?" he greeted harshly. "Surprised you'd show yourself around my place at all."

"It's me," Dubose nodded, reining in. Neither he nor Ragley dismounted but sat quietly in their saddles. "Pete and me here, we come looking for some Y-J horses that run loose. Tracks started in this direction."

"Ain't seen no stray horses," Ike said.

"Waal, too bad." Still they sat, killing time. Smith's gun was angled across his left arm, ready for quick work. "Aimin' to pick off a deer with yore gun, maybe, Smith? Right here from the front porch?"

The law of hospitality was a strong one out West, but Smith was far from hospitable in manner, and Dubose was subtly hinting at this, grinning.

"You want anything else?" Smith countered.

"Nawp, reckon not. Just resting and thinking a bit. Right long spell of dry weather we been having, ain't it?"

"You didn't come here to be sociable, Dubose."

"Any reason why two honest ranchers couldn't be sociable?"

Smith eyed him intently, wondering. Dubose calmly chewed tobacco and waited. Pete Ragley was taut and motionless like a coiled steel spring. For a quarter of an hour more, Dubose bluffed and Smith tried to figure it out. Finally Dubose straightened in his saddle, slowly raised both his arms in a stretch and a yawn. This was a pre-arranged signal.

From the side of Smith's house a lasso snaked out with whiplike speed. Its loop was small. It settled around Ike Smith's body and arms and was jerked tight in a split second, tieing his elbows to his ribs and causing the rifle to fall.

Smith was cursing in sheer astonishment. But in that same moment Pete Ragley had leaped from his horse and run forward with a piggin' string. It was exactly as if he and Karpe were a team of calf ropers at a rodeo; Karpe's lasso had gone over the victim's head, and now Pete was tieing him hand and foot. Dubose sat calmly watching it until the two cowboys stood up, faces flaming.

Dubose spat. "Now Smith," he drawled, "it's clear why we come here. Me and these boys just killed and skun a steer back yonder on your land. It had your brand on the outside, but it had an older brand—mine—on the inside. You been selling many more steers than your breed cows could produce. But you're done, here and now."

Karpe was knotting another lariat rope, not to form a loop this time, but a noose.

"It ain't no tree handy, men," Dubose lamented. "But there's open rafters inside his shack here."

Smith began pleading, talking, promising, begging in every way he knew. He'd sign any sort of papers. He'd pay all his cash. He'd deed all his land to them. He'd get out of the country forever.

"You'll get out of the country, all right," Karpe growled. "You're getting out right now."

They made no more ceremony than was actually necessary to drag him inside, stand on a chair, and pass the rope over a rafter some ten feet high. Then the three men heaved on the rope and lifted Ike Smith, dangling by the neck.

The last words Smith heard on this earth were, "You're getting what all rustlers deserve."

The three Y-J men rode home, then. The next day they went in to Vinegaroon, and Judge Bean with some helpers, including big Bart Gobble, his personal assistant, went out to bring in Smith's body. The Judge also picked up a branding iron near Smith's house. It was a long rod with a pretty design on the end, the Three-leaf Clover. And at the official hearing of the evidence there on the Bean front porch, which served as coroner's courtroom, Bean himself showed the several citizens gathered about what Smith had done with the clover iron.

"He'd made his iron to match the size of Mr. Dubose's Yes Jenny," Bean said. "He got what was coming to him."

Smith had burned the clover over the Y-J Connected this way:

It was easy to do, and it would never show from the outside, hence he could burn it over stolen Y-J stock by the hundreds. But any burned-over brand shows on the inside, if you trouble to kill the animal and study the first brand.

Judge Bean closed the case officially when he put the clover-leaf iron inside the coffin with Ike Smith and closed the lid. There are other clover-leaf brands today in good repute in West Texas. But that particular one went underground in the infamy it deserved.

9

FEUD FURY

JUST AT SUNSET on a gently sloping hillside in northern Arizona, a sheepherder was preparing a lonely meal. Within sight of his fire his herd lay resting, quietly bedding down for the night. The scene was a tranquil one, a setting old in the memory of man long before Christ was born. Everything seemed at peace. Bacon was frying in the herder's tiny skillet. Coffee in his smoke-blackened pot had just begun to boil, when with no warning a rifle shot broke the calm.

The bullet ripped through the pot of coffee and knocked the frying pan off the fire. Hot coals sizzled as coffee poured over them.

Instantly the herder jumped aside and fell prone behind a boulder. His own gun cocked now, he peered cautiously in all directions. For an hour or more he watched, his hunger forgotten. When the light of his fire finally died down, he stealthily gathered his meager equipment and slipped away.

Thus in the year of 1887 began the bloodiest feud in the history of western America, the sanguinary war between the Grahams and the Tewksburys which did not end until the "last man" was left with nobody to shoot and with nobody to shoot at him.

Reverberations of the feud are heard each fall and spring, when sheep are being moved to and from the lowlands of the Southwest. Wherever sheep and cattle raisers get together

132

tales are told of this greatest of range wars. More than a hundred motion pictures and perhaps twice that many novels
and short stories have been based on it. Authors are prone to
"discover" it and go overboard with enthusiasm—Zane Gray,
notably, who used it in his novel *To The Last Man*. South-
westerners have come to take a certain pride in the feud because of its sheer ferocity and its colorful detail. It will stand
forever as one of the few really shocking wild-western epics.

The feud has been named, incongruously enough, the
Pleasant Valley War. It was far from pleasant; the name, of
course, is geographic. Most of the bloody events took place
within that idyllic area just under the Mogollon Rim known
as Pleasant Valley. The postoffice is called Young.

Mogollon Rim (pronounce it Mo-go-yone') is a long
cliff formation, *below* which the sheepherder was making
his camp near his animals that night. The word "below" is
important, because had he camped above, the shot would
never have been fired, and perhaps the feud would never
have materialized.

In bringing sheep to graze below the rim the herder had
broken an unwritten law laid down by cattlemen of Pleasant
Valley, where the grass was luscious and rich and the water
was plentiful. The cattlemen, who despised and hated anyone who would "sink so low as to raise sheep," had issued
warnings that sheep must stay to the north, in the highlands,
and that none would be tolerated past the geographic border,
the Rim.

Among the leading residents of Pleasant Valley and the
surrounding territory were the Graham brothers and J. D.
Tewksbury. They and their families had established ranches
there in the early eighteen eighties in defiance of hostile Indians. At first, the nearest white settlement was one hundred
miles away. The region knew absolutely no law, save the
law of might and main, of rifle and pistol, of fists and knife.

A common interest—defense against the marauding Indians —therefore made nominal friendship necessary between the two clans for a time.

But other settlers came in, and as the years passed enmity developed between the Grahams and the Tewksburys. The two factions began to accuse each other of cattle rustling, and from petty causes bad feeling arose.

One peculiarly dramatic episode foretold the beginning of the Pleasant Valley War. Two young men aligned with the opposing factions made frequent youthful boasts about their prowess in combat. Each made it clear that not only could he strangle and kill the other on sight, but that he would welcome the first opportunity to do so. They were two roosters with long spurs, eager to fight.

The Graham supporter was Tobias Blevins. The correct name of the Tewksbury supporter, who is said to have been a half-blood, is now a matter of disagreement; he was known as Ed Kyle. The two were so persistent in their threats against each other that disinterested parties finally took action.

The frontier citizens caught both men, stripped them down to their underwear, gave each one a sharp bowie knife, and locked them in an unfurnished and utterly dark one-room cabin.

Eventually Blevins crawled out alone, with a long gash across his face and smaller ones on his body. He disappeared from the community without further delay, because angered Tewksburys would doubtless have finished what his luckless opponent had not. A "fair" fight was not the consideration in this bloody range war; rather was it a case of eye for eye, regardless of cause.

Tom Graham, a grand-appearing man with handsome features, a firm chin, a black beard and mustache, and fists like knots of steel, and also an expert horseman and a dead shot with any firearm, seemed automatically to drift into the leadership of the Graham faction. Tom it was who issued the blunt warnings to sheepherders to keep their contemptible woollies in the highlands.

But sheep raisers eyed the rich grass in Pleasant Valley with envy. Knowing that all range was free to him who took it, two men essayed to bring a large herd down. They were the Daggs brothers, and one of their herders was a dependable Navaho. It was this Indian whose coffee pot was so abruptly punctured as he prepared his evening meal.

With this warning the Daggs brothers sought armed protection before they made their next move. They hired members of the friendly Tewksbury family to guard their herd when next they tried to enter the forbidden valley.

From that point on things happened fast and furiously. Today one may count nearly thirty graves of the feudists on Pleasant Valley ranches, and nobody will ever know how many participants in the war were buried in places unknown.

The Grahams, headed by Tom, had laid down a law, established a deadline, and shot at a herder's campfire. The Daggs brothers, aided by the Tewksburys, then sent in a big herd of sheep under heavy guard as a direct challenge.

The news spread like a forest fire. Cattlemen everywhere, and sheepmen as well, rallied to one standard or the other. Many were honest, peace-loving men who subsequently fought and died without knowing the true cause of the trouble. Some cattlemen joined the Tewksburys, but mostly they stuck by Tom Graham.

Every week saw a growing spirit of resentment. The Indian herder was killed from ambush. Neither side paid much attention to that, for the life of an Indian was held of little more worth than that of a dog. Nevertheless, he was a Tewksbury employee.

Enraged cowboys slipped into herds of sheep at night and killed many animals, shooting them and driving flocks of them over cliffs to mass destruction. The Tewksburys vainly sought for the guilty men, rounded up more supporters, and swore vengeance.

The Graham faction was aided by a group of tough cowboys who comprised the Aztec Land and Cattle Company, nicknamed the Hash Knife Outfit. The nickname arose from the shape of its cattle brand but also reflected the character of its men. They were fierce fighters, crack shots, adventure-loving pioneers.

Then the first white men in the feud were killed. "Old Man" Blevins—his full name has been forgotten, but it is believed to have been John—disappeared.

Four "Hashers" and four Grahams started a search for Blevins, a Graham friend. They rode hard all morning. Noon brought them to the Middleton ranchhouse. Still mounted, the eight men called through an ominous silence that enveloped the cabins. Presently a woman came to the door, opening it just enough to poke her head through.

"I cain't give you no vittles, they ain't nothin' to eat here." She refused their request in a surly manner and in direct violation of the firmly established pioneer law of hospitality. Surprised, but not yet suspicious, the hungry men looked at each other, then turned their horses to ride away.

Without warning, a volley of rifle shots came from the house. Horses screamed in fright and pain. Confusion enveloped the Graham partisans, and two of them, Hamp Blevins and John Payne, toppled to the ground. A third, G. T. Tucker, fell mortally wounded.

The five other horsemen drew their pistols and fired haphazardly at the ranch-house windows while retreating. No one knows whether their volley did any harm. And no-

body knows exactly who was in the house and fired the dastardly shots from ambush.

Edwin and James Tewksbury were accused of being the leaders, however. Certainly, they were the logical persons to suspect of complicity in the slaughter. The Grahams began a determined search, and a careful one, for them.

Members of both factions, for that matter, began a purposeful hunt for one another. The details of this tense and dramatic moment in the war have been described by an eyewitness to much of it—a man who would have made all of them stop fighting if he could. He was Hamilcar "Sinkiller" Pool, a pioneer preacher who was plenty rough and rugged himself because he had to be, but who deplored unnecessary killing.

"They hated each other with a fierce passion," he said in 1930, of the Grahams and Tewksburys. "After that ambush at the Middleton ranch nothing could stop them. I tried it and nearly got shot for my trouble. Both sides accused me of being friends of the other. My own life was in danger.

"Everybody's life was in constant danger, in fact, whether you was taking part in the war or not. You took your life in your hands if you rode down a forest trail. Like as not, somebody would put a bullet in your back from behind a tree, and you nor nobody else would ever know who done it. Your body would just be found, and somebody would have to bury it."

Ambush and ambuscade, sniping and sneaking, pitched battles between gangs, individual fights to the death—that was the order of things for several weeks. And then William Graham, eighteen-year-old brother of Tom, was shot to death by J. D. Houck, a Tewksbury partisan.

William was the first Graham to die in the feud. Members of the Graham "army"—that is, friends and partisans—had died, but no actual member of the family. Little William's death infuriated big brother Tom and made him a devil of wrath and vindictiveness.

Tom at once laid plans to wipe out the entire Tewksbury clan in one big battle, to lay one determined siege that would end the bloody war and bring him ample revenge.

There followed the climax of the first two phases of the great war between the Grahams and the Tewksburys, a climax which is now conceded to be the most terrible single episode of its sort in western history. The sheer horror of it brought the first intervention from an outside source, from authorized law and order.

One morning Tom Graham collected all his men and quietly surrounded the ranch house and corrals of the Tewksburys before the latter were aware of what was going on. On their own home ranch, where enemies would hardly dare to show themselves, the Tewksburys evidently reasoned that extreme caution was not necessary; therefore, no sentinels had been posted.

John Tewksbury and a partisan named Jacobs were

walking a short distance from the house that morning when the concealed Grahams and their henchmen opened fire. The Tewksbury men fell in their tracks on an open hillside, not far from troughs where hogs were eating.

At once shots were fired into the ranch home, and in a few seconds the house was converted into a fortress bristling with guns. Several members of the family were inside, together with some of the ranch workmen. They made loopholes of cracks in walls, windows, and doors and searched the outside landscape for human targets.

But the Graham targets were hard to find. They had concealed themselves carefully behind rocks and shrubbery, whence they were able to keep careful watch on the house without endangering themselves.

A man darted suddenly from the house toward the bodies of Jacobs and John Tewksbury, bent evidently on bringing them in or rendering them aid if not too late. Bullets nicked him at once and he fled back inside to die of his wounds.

For hours the situation held; no person could leave the ranchhouse without drawing fire from Graham rifles.

Late in the morning, ugly, grunting, eternally hungry porkers waddled from their troughs over to the bodies of the slain men. The sniping stopped; both sides seemed to pause in order to behold the horror. The hogs proceeded with their ghoulish business, and in a moment somebody within the house shouted a plea.

"Graham, will you give us a chance to get those bodies?"

A volley of shots was the only answer.

Thinking that perhaps the attackers had not heard the request, and hoping that out of ordinary human decency they would permit him to bury the bodies, another Tewksbury partisan tried to leave the ranchhouse. He was shot down before he had the door wide open.

Defenders of the ranch sniped as best they could at the

prowling hogs and did in some measure delay their ghastly work, killing many of them that approached the bodies. But ammunition was precious. Other hogs came, and it was soon evident that the slain men must eventually be devoured entirely, in full view of relatives and friends.

The situation was intolerable to the widow of John Tewksbury, and she took bold action. With no warning at all she threw open the front door of her home and walked bravely out, defying the attacking Grahams to kill her. She carried no gun; her head was held high. She did not run; she walked, determinedly, straight toward her husband's body.

Miraculously, her act of incredible bravery touched the streak of chivalry inherent in all pioneer men, however tough and vindictive they may be. Not a single shot was fired from the moment she opened the door until she returned. While the eyes of both parties followed her, she quietly covered the bodies and walked back to the house.

The slamming of the door behind her was the signal for instant volleys from both "armies." Bullets splattered everywhere as the fighting was resumed with greater and more devastating fury.

The siege lasted for several days and would probably have been fought to a finish if news of it had not been rushed to the office of the nearest sheriff, in Prescott. One morning Deputy Sheriff Meadows and a strong posse arrived unexpectedly at the scene and forced the Grahams to retire.

Their arrival brought a momentary lull in the feud and marked the end of the "first half" of the fighting. Nobody ever knew how many were killed and injured in that attack on the Tewksbury ranch, and accounts given now by old timers in the region vary; but at least a dozen are known to have fallen.

The large number of deaths, plus the horrible mutilation of the two bodies, caused a wave of resentment against both warring factions. It is likely, too, that both sides had had enough fighting for the time; so the tenseness subsided and the shooting ceased.

But not the resentment. This lull, which many persons hoped was the end of the Pleasant Valley War, turned out to be a mere resting period. Soon bullets were flying faster than ever.

During the recess in actual gun-fighting, however, an odd phase developed. Men and women of both parties lived side by side in the same town, Prescott, seeing each other every day, meeting in stores and courtrooms, rubbing elbows on the streets, but never speaking a word to each other. Meantime, the law penetrated into Pleasant Valley, and each side shifted the battle from the rifle range to the courts. Each faction began to accuse the other of every sort of crime—cattle rustling, horse thieving, sheep killing, arson, and murder. Formal warrants for one man or more would be sworn out in legal fashion, and all the routine of court machinery would then be opened. Whole families would strap pistols to their belts and go watch the court proceedings. Night and day the town was loaded with dynamite ready to explode at the least untoward action. Workaday citizens were afraid to go out on the streets.

The inevitable explosion which caused the resumption of bloodshed occurred in an adjoining county, near the little town of Holbrook, Arizona. Here the majesty of the law was capably upheld by Sheriff Commodore Owens. Commodore (his real name) looked the part of a wild West sheriff—big and dark, wearing boots, a high hat, and sometimes a leather suit, and always a six-shooter or two in full view. He was a man who knew no fear and who could shoot a rifle or a pistol from his hip with as much accuracy as from his shoulder—a feat that is rare indeed.

A man named Andy Cooper, who owned some cattle

in Pleasant Valley and was a cohort of the Grahams, had been accused time and again of cattle stealing. But he was cagey about his rustling, so no direct evidence could be found against him.

Eventually the grand jury issued an indictment against Cooper, but with the whispered admission that it was largely a bluff; it was hoped that evidence would develop after his arrest. To Sheriff Owens fell the duty of bringing the rustler to book.

Commodore did not rush into it. Biding his time, he hoped to gather his evidence first. Known as a Tewksbury sympathizer, but not actually a participant in the war, the sheriff tried to play fair and do his duty as an officer of the law. But the loafers and bartenders in the frontier saloons at Holbrook began to bait him and accuse him of being afraid of Cooper. He ignored these taunts at first, but one Saturday the loafers made him so miserable with their talk that he became exasperated.

"By the eternal, I'll show you if I'm afraid to arrest him!" the sheriff roared, as he mounted his horse to ride away.

It was known that Cooper was staying that day with his mother, Mrs. John Blevins, a Grahamite, in her cabin a short distance from Holbrook. Moreover, Owens knew that Cooper was a dangerous man and a killer if need be. But the sheriff approached the cabin alone in broad daylight. Dismounting in the front yard, he strode forward and rapped on the door. Cooper himself opened it.

"What do you want?" he growled at the sheriff.

"I've come for you, Andy. You are under arrest and you must come with me," replied the officer.

"Well, wait just a minute." And Cooper disappeared inside the cabin again.

Some intuition made Commodore Owens suspicious, so he backed away from the door toward his horse, holding his cocked rifle pointed at the cabin. His hunch was not a bad one.

In a flash the door was jerked open and a rifle cracked. The ball whizzed past Owens' head and killed his horse.

Then followed one of the strangest and bloodiest battles in the Pleasant Valley War—a one-man siege by an unprotected man against a cabin containing three men, a boy, and a woman, all armed. The odds were tremendously against Commodore, but no man in all Arizona was a better shot than he.

Before the door closed Owens shot his rifle from the hip and hit his would-be murderer in the chest.

In another second his keen eye saw Cooper peering at him through a crack in the window, and he instantly put a rifle bullet through the wall boarding just below the window. Cooper groaned and fell dying with a wound in his abdomen.

In another twinkling of an eye a man named Mose Roberts appeared around an outside corner of the cabin, holding a revolver ready and drawing a bead on Owens.

Once more Owens' rifle spoke, still from the hip, before Roberts could pull his own trigger. Roberts crawled back into the cabin and died within ten minutes.

At this juncture only sixteen-year-old Sam Blevins and his mother were left standing inside. Infuriated by the failure of his elders, the youth grasped a pistol and dashed out the door, his mother crying hysterically and clinging to him. Sheriff Owens beheld this move calmly, standing motionless, his deadly rifle cocked and aimed in its hip position.

Young Blevins raised his gun to fire, and Owens squeezed his trigger. The boy scarcely knew what hit him, for Owens' bullet pierced his heart.

From that point on no more evidence of life came from within the cabin, save for groans and the cries of the woman.

Sheriff Owens backed cautiously away and was gone.

Men sent to investigate found the place a veritable shambles.

"Blood was all over the floor, the furniture, and the walls," one of the investigators said. "I never saw such a terrible sight in all my life."

Sheriff Commodore Owens, in many ways the most picturesque of all the frontier officers, died at the town of Seligman, Arizona, in 1919, from a common illness. But from the day of that one-man siege, nobody again accused him of cowardice.

This wiping out of four members of the Graham faction naturally did not set well with its fierce leader, Tom Graham. Still the Grahams could not, or would not, openly assault the sheriff who wielded his rifle with such deadly effect. Despite his affiliation with the Tewksburys, Owens was an officer of the law, and the law was enjoying growing strength and prestige. Best kill Owens from ambush, Graham reasoned—but he never realized this hope.

However, in the succeeding months many a man did die from ambush on both sides. One day Cart Jenkins, a sheepman and hence a Tewksbury clansman, started from his rural home on horseback. At nightfall his horse returned riderless. Tied to the saddle horn was part of a sheep hide soaked in human blood. Two days later Jenkins' body was found, with the remaining part of the sheep skin thrown over it.

Mario Contreras, a Mexican herder who had fought with the Tewksburys, arose one morning to find his entire flock of woollies piled dead and dying at the foot of a sheer rock cliff a mile from his camp. Doubtless cursing himself for being a sound sleeper. Contreras trailed his beasts to the cliff's edge and peered over at the scene of destruction below. At that instant a rifle cracked from ambush, and the hapless shepherd fell six hundred feet and more to join his flock.

One day at sunrise a man named Hockery or Hockaway opened the front door of his cabin, and instantly a rifle bullet pierced his brain. He died on the spot.

Sheriff William Mulvernon from Yavapai County next led a posse into Pleasant Valley, promising to arrest the leaders in the feud. For some reason that has never become apparent, he directed virtually all his efforts toward the Graham faction. No evidence has ever shown that Sheriff Mulvernon was a Tewksbury man, so perhaps he was misled about the facts.

He and his posse learned that Charles Blevins and John Graham were awaiting them in a cabin not far from a little village store. Mulvernon resorted to a bit of trickery. He rode with his men to the store and inquired for Blevins and Graham. Upon being informed that they were not present, the posse openly galloped away, as if leaving the scene entirely. Then the possemen all crept back and concealed themselves behind an old wall and other breastworks near the store. In due course Blevins and Graham left their cabin and rode to the store to get a report on the posse's call. They were all well armed, but evidently not suspicious. When they were within range, the sheriff spoke.

"Graham, we've got you covered! You and Blevins throw up your hands and don't move!"

But the sheriff should never have hoped for his command to be obeyed as easily as that. Blevins and Graham were hard men accustomed to danger, who gave no quarter and expected none. In a flash they wheeled their horses and spurred them, drew their pistols, and fired in the direction of the sheriff's voice. Simultaneously a half-dozen rifles spoke, and both Blevins and Graham toppled off their horses dead.

The official posse then milled around the community a bit, arrested two Tewksburys and later released them, and finally went on back home, having done little good in halting the war. Thereafter the feud settled down to another spell of ambush and individual murders.

Two boys and a man, whose names are now recalled as Wilson, Stott, and Scott, all Graham partisans, were caught in the forest one day and accused of an imaginary crime by the Tewksburys. Then they were all hanged from the same tree. Any number of hangings were committed in just that manner by both sides. (Hanging has ever been a favorite "outdoor sport" among the wild element of southwestern society.) The sniping, hanging, and fighting kept on until only one member of each family was left alive. These were Tom Graham and Ed Tewksbury. The last Graham to die before Tom was James, a brother who passed away from natural causes.

Tom Graham admitted that he was tired of bloodshed and had no desire to carry on the feud. He announced publicly that he was done with fighting, done with trying to raise cattle in Pleasant Valley, and that he was going to move away.

And so he did. He unstrapped his guns and never thereafter went armed, despite the pleas of his wife and friends. He moved into southern Arizona to the little farming town of Tempe, near Phoenix. There he planted a crop of wheat and barley and set about to end his days as a law-abiding citizen. Without their leader, and with the Tewksburys also tired of fighting, the Graham henchmen disbanded, and it seemed that the long and bloody war was at an end.

So far as Pleasant Valley was concerned, it was. But it cropped up in one final ugly thrust in southern Arizona, where it had followed Tom Graham.

He was riding to town one sunny day on top of a wagonload of barley, driving his mules along the Twin Buttes road. Right in front of the Twin Buttes schoolhouse a shot was fired from ambush. Hit in the back, Tom fell over dead.

Two school children had seen the murder and, much frightened, ran to tell their parents that men resembling Edward Tewksbury and his friend John Rhodes had been hiding behind a clump of bushes and that Rhodes had fired the fatal shot. A posse took up their trail and soon arrested both culprits.

Quite a hullabaloo was raised over this renewal of the sheep-and-cattle feud. In the valley around Tempe and Phoenix, the farmers were much incensed at such doings and demanded that the courts exact full justice in the case of the guilty men.

The trial was a long-drawn-out wrangle. Rhodes, charged with first-degree murder, worked up an alibi. Tewksbury was also able to "prove" through a cowboy witness that he was miles from the scene of the murder when it was committed. But the children were steadfast in their claims. Feudist retribution was very nearly exacted against Rhodes before he even came to trial, during his preliminary hearing. He stood before the justice of the peace who was questioning him. Among the plaintiffs appeared the widow of the slain man. Mrs. Graham, dressed in black and wearing a black shawl, sobbed throughout the legal proceedings and meanwhile edged quietly toward Rhodes.

Suddenly and without warning she drew a pistol from her shawl, poked the muzzle of it in Rhodes's side, and pulled the trigger. Fate stepped in and thwarted her, however. The hammer caught in the strands of her shawl, and the revolver failed to go off.

Rhodes' luck stayed with him. After a change of venue, a second trial ended in prolonged disagreement, and eventually both he and Tewksbury were set free. Nobody knows what became of Tewksbury; Rhodes died a few years later of tuberculosis.

Thus Ed Tewksbury was the "last man"—the last actual participant in this, the bloodiest, the most vindictive feud in western American history.[1]

[1] The student of southwestern history will note discrepancies between any two accounts of the Pleasant Valley feud. Knowing that no written records were kept and that word-of-mouth reports are always faulty and in this instance outrageously biased, I have simply related the various episodes as they are commonly told and have tried to maintain a middle ground in dealing both with the sensational aspects and with the guilt or innocence of the two factions.

10

HI JOLLY AND THE CAMELS

DAWN WAS just lifting its great velvet curtain on the vast stage formed by the prairies of Texas, when a strange new scent rode in on a gentle breeze.

"Oo-o-om?" one steer rumbled, querulously.

The steer was one of nearly three thousand cattle bedded down on the long trail to northern markets. That first weird bellow caused hundreds of other heads to lift, snorting. Off to the right, a cowboy caught the warning and sang a little louder, trying to soothe his charges. On this trek nothing unusual had happened for five days, which in itself was cause for worry.

"BAWR-R-R-R!"

This time it was a primeval clarion, a wilderness alarm. The herd leaped to its feet with a roar like rolling thunder. Whatever scent rode the breeze now came potent and strong and frightening; every steer saw death itself in the growing shades of dawn. The thunder swelled, and the cattle fanned out in a frenzy of running. A dust cloud rose. Brush was trampled, and small trees were knocked down. A horse was gored, and a pair of snooping coyotes were run down and literally ground to pieces by the running hoofs. Ben Cariker, a Negro cowboy, was knocked out of his saddle and took refuge in an oak near by. Two Mexican vaqueros saved their lives by diving off an embankment into a river, but since the water was only two feet deep they were badly hurt. The bank was an overhang, and they crouched back in safety while frenzied cattle poured over and stacked up before their eyes.

Though half a mile away from the herd's bed-ground, the chuck wagon was knocked over and broken beyond repair. Saddles, bedrolls, harness, guns—all manner of trail equipment was scattered and destroyed in this great excitement, which is still called the worst cattle stampede in Texas history.

The stampede occurred in 1857 and had a strange cause, one never known before and never repeated. That weird scent on the breeze had come all the way from Arabia. And the man immediately responsible for it was the only "spectator" at this extraordinary stampede. His name was Hadj Ali, and throughout the excitement he remained quite calm.

As a matter of fact, he rode right through the middle of the panic on a sort of grandstand seat. He took no action simply because he didn't know what was going on. His mount was one of several capable saddle animals, and they too refused to be distracted by the fantastic bellowing and running of the Texas steers. They just acted aloof, even bored, and went plodding on at a fast walk over the prairie.

The stampede lasted most of two days. The steers were scattered so far and wide and their fright was so great that they covered part of four counties, and hundreds literally ran themselves to death. Three of the eighteen cowboys in the trail party were not seen again for months because of injuries and assorted superstitions. The monetary damage caused by the maddened cattle never fully was estimated.

The morning of the third day, the trail boss, Alec P. Granger, a former Kentuckian, huddled with what remained of his crew.

"This here is the damndest thing I ever heard tell of," he

announced flatly. "Five, six, you fellows swear you seen a vision."

"I did," one chap nodded.

"I seen it," another was emphatic.

"Alec," a third put in, "I keep a-tellin' you it was camels. I know what a camel is. I've seen pitchers, and I can read. So help me, when I topped that little hill over to the west that morning, I seen a man settin' on top of a camel's hump!"

"Hell!" the trail boss snorted.

"I ain't lyin'! He was settin' up there ridin' along like the pitcher of the wise men in Ma's Bible back home. And that ain't all. Behind him was a string of other camels, some with packsaddles on. They wasn't paying me no attention, nor the steers either. They just walked on fast."

Other men nodded solemnly. The boss swore. He told them they had all gone stark crazy. He called them names. He almost got into gunplay—until they took him six miles away and showed him the tracks. They were unlike any tracks he had ever seen before.

That dramatic introduction of Hadj Ali and his camels into the United States also introduces the strangest, and funniest, chapter of southwestern history. Moreover, it is a relatively unknown chapter. Strangers hearing it for the first time are wont to grin broadly and start a counterattack with yarns about talking fish, two-headed snakes, and such. They think the narrator is as sun-touched as the trail boss back there thought his cowboys were. If the reader harbors any such skepticism, let him check into the records of the United States government, for no less a personage than Uncle Sam himself was responsible for our camels. They soon became white elephants—a strange metamorphosis, considering the nature of the beasts—and as such they colored our regional legend in a unique manner.

Camels are not native to this continent. However, parts

of the American Southwest have a climate much like that of the desert in Asia and Africa. In 1856 Jefferson Davis, then secretary of war, conceived a bright idea. The army was having trouble with the Indians out West, and always a major problem was the transporting of arms and supplies. He learned that camels could travel about twice as far in a day as pack mules or horses and could carry even heavier loads.

"The thing to do," said Mr. Davis, "is import a herd of camels and put them to work in the Southwest. It will be cheaper and better in the long run."

The idea had real brilliance, on paper. Congress appropriated the money, and Lieutenant David Porter, of the United States Navy, was sent to Smyrna to buy thirty-four camels and hire drivers who knew how to handle them. In due time he sailed back with his cargo, landing at Indianola, Texas. Nine baby camels had been born en route, so Hadj Ali as boss cameleer started westward with forty-three "ships of the desert." Their destination was New Mexico, where the sands begin, but Hadj unwittingly crossed the cattle trail.

The great stampede was only the beginning of events involving those camels and their placid Mohammedan driver. Indeed, for almost sixty-five years they left their imprint on the West, although as an experiment in American transportation they were a complete failure. And the failure itself was caused largely by the temperament of the westerners.

At the Bar-X-Bar Ranch in New Mexico, Hadj Ali paused to rest. He put his camels in a pasture, which was rented from a woman because the men of the ranch were away at the time. The camels calmly stepped over a fence that evening and ambled into a barn to eat some fresh hay they had smelled there. At midnight the men of the ranch returned "likkered up" from an excursion into town—not drunk, but hilarious. The first man went into the barn to throw feed down . . . and came bang on to the humpbacked animals.

"Whe-e-euw!" He let out a sighing kind of whistle and backed outside. He was too inarticulate to report what he had seen. The others, sensing trouble, drew their six-shooters and crept around to windows and doors. When they peered in, they also fell back in high suspicion of their own senses.

In one body they raced for their horses again, mounted, and galloped back to town. They didn't return to the ranch until the sun was high the next morning, and by then Hadj Ali and his strange caravan had gone. The woman, according to War Department records, was paid five dollars for that night's camel board.

In due time, Hadj Ali reported to his employers at an army outpost in New Mexico, and the camels were promptly put to work. At least, an attempt was made to put them to work. An experienced mule skinner named McLemore was their first American nurse, and he went at his job in a characteristic if sullen manner.

"All right, you ornery sons of Satan," he roared at the loaded caravan that first morning, "let's git out'a heah. Giddap!"

Not a camel moved. "Giddap" was not in the Arabian vocabulary. Nor was any of the classic assortment of profanity which Mule Skinner McLemore then showered upon them.

In desperation, Mac unlimbered a blacksnake whip and cracked the rump of the nearest camel. The indignant beast swung his long neck around and—this, too, is on record—spat squarely and profusely in Mr. McLemore's face. Moreover, it lowered its head, humped its hump a foot higher, and charged the man pell-mell!

Mac did what any sensible man would have done. And

as he ran, some dozen other men burst into hearty guffaws. From the top of a stockade post Mac told the camels and the cockeyed world what he thought of the whole business. It was a fine speech, during which he resigned his job.

In the weeks he spent traveling on the ocean and across Texas, Hadj Ali had learned bits of English, and he could get along in conversation fairly well now. But his own name had been translated euphoniously by the westerners into the version that will stand on the records forever. It appears even over his grave, a simple mispronunciation of his real name. The Americans made it "Hi Jolly."

He was friendly and honest and therefore popular. When a mule skinner had trouble—and many more besides Mc-Lemore did—the other Americans would uproariously side with Hi. Poems and songs were created about Hi Jolly. He didn't understand the songs, but he liked the people. He tried valiantly to teach them how to handle his camels, how to get work out of them, how to love them somewhat as a cowboy loves his horse. But you can't go up to a camel, slap him on the shoulder, and say, "Ho, you old piebald cussword, let's git to ridin'." A camel simply doesn't understand such language or familiarity.

The War Department continued to receive adverse reports on the adaptability of the camels. They were strong beasts, but strange. No American could get along with them, and nobody wanted to ride up on a hump, anyway. Hi Jolly was faithful, but he couldn't herd the animals across the wilderness trails forever.

Rapidly the fame of the humped quadrupeds spread, and everywhere they caused both hilarity and trouble. No rancher wanted to pasture them, after news of the first experiences spread. And tragedy struck one day, when the queer caravan caused a horse to go loco and buck off a surly rancher.

The rancher, J. A. Strode, rounded up some of his henchmen and set out to get vengeance. The general reputation of
his gang bunch was none too savory, anyway, and this time
they lived up to it. Creeping near the camp of Hadj Ali at
night, they suddenly pounced upon a sleeping form.

The form was Hi Jolly right enough, but he came up
swinging an Arabian knife. Then a gun fired. Hi realized his
danger, threw his knife at the nearest man, and fled into a
clump of trees near by. A few minutes later in the moonlight the mob ran down a man they thought was the cameleer,
looped a rope around his neck and dragged him to death
over the rocks. This was about half a mile from the camels'
bed-ground.

"Now let's go back and kill the stinking camels!" one rancher cried.

They set out to do just that, but Hi Jolly had remained loyal to his herd. While they pursued and lynched the man they believed was the Mohammedan but was really a bearded Mexican helper, Hi had cut back to the animals and escaped with them up a canyon.

Hi Jolly's knife had done some damage, too; as a result of his throw a man named Bullton wore a scar on his face the rest of his time. Bullton was well known in Bisbee, Arizona, as recently as 1910, and he often told of the camel disturbances.

Trouble with the westerners, however, was just one of the camels' trials and tribulations. Another important drawback to their use—one not foreseen by Secretary Jefferson Davis, was that the southwestern desert region is generally covered with rocks, whereas the Arabian and Egyptian deserts are composed primarily of fine sand. Rocks cut the softly padded hoofs of the camels and often left them crippled. It was infeasible to shoe them as horses and mules are shod.

Therefore, the experiment was soon termed a failure, and the federal government admitted as much. But the camels were there, and so was Hi Jolly.

"I have done what I contracted to do," Hi announced. "Now I like this country, and I shall make it my home. But I want no more of the camels." He became an honorable citizen and lived in his adopted land until his death in 1902. He is buried near Quartzite, Arizona, under a stone pyramid topped with a camel in copper silhouette.

After his retirement from herding the humped brutes, the excitement and legends really began. The government offered the camels for sale. But who would have one? A few sportive souls willing to gamble on anything each bought one of the camels. They had their fun. Jean Cretin, of French birth, thought he could use them for freighting ore up in Nevada, so he bought most of them for a song. He lost money on that deal and moved the herd to Florence, Arizona, on another packing venture. There Jean died, without heirs.

"What'll we do with these blankety-blank beasts?" the local magistrate demanded of the undertaker.

"I have no responsibility," said the mortician. "I will not touch them."

"You're the last one touched Cretin," the law ruled. "Them camels are yours."

By night the frightened mortician simply removed the halters from the camels and yelled "shoo!" at them. They all shooed. In due time they had shooed over four states and built for themselves reputations that still endure.

One day Hosteen Begay, a young Navaho Indian employed by white men at Globe, Arizona, came face to face with two of the freed ruminants in a mountain gorge. He had been a steady, reliable Indian theretofore, but that day he dropped his miner's pick, forgot all about his rifle, tent, food, and the silver he had been mining, and started off at a hard run. He ran all the way to the Navaho reservation, without stopping at all, some swear, a distance of two hundred miles or more. No one ever could persuade him to leave it again.

Hunters and trappers began to report the darndest tales imaginable. One day Tod Cartwright, a buffalo and elk specialist, hurried wild-eyed into a village. "I seen it!" he roared "I ain't had a drink in two months, but I seen it!"

"You seen what?" a citizen demanded.

"A hump-shouldered elk with no antlers! It was twelve foot high and had a neck like a swan!"

Uncle Tod was slightly excited but reasonably accurate. The folks tried to kid him, whereupon he opened his packs and produced a large, odorous animal skin. It was unlike any hide anybody around there had ever seen.

These good people hadn't heard about the camels, and they concluded that Uncle Tod Cartwright had really soared to hunter's heights. His fame long outlived him.

Down in the desert region some twenty miles from Phoenix, Nature had erected a camel that is some twelve hundred feet high. It is the nearly perfect form of a camel, kneeling down, with its long neck and head stretched out as if sleeping. Of course, it is renowned as a landmark, under the name Camelback Mountain, and sure enough, the real camels drifted out that way and precipitated more odd episodes.

One day a Mexican boy lassoed one of the strange beasts. It came along peaceably enough. The boy debated what to do with his catch, then remembered something and led it toward Phoenix. He called near sundown at the home of Joe Porterie, an assayer.

"Señor Porterie," the lad began, "wan time you loan me the monee, the ten dollar. I breeng you thees camel to pay for him."

Porterie was astonished, but he was a good sport and reasoned, no doubt, that even a camel was better payment than nothing on a bad loan. So he took the strange beast's rope and at once started for town to sell him. Quite naturally, he headed for the popular Bon Ton Saloon. Some forty or fifty citizens gathered around Porterie and his camel.

"Well, well!" one gent roared. "What ya' gonna do with him, Joe?"

"Will he give milk?" another demanded.

"Can he sing?" asked a third.

Joe Porterie's genial grin began to fade. Jibes and laughter peppered him from every side. The sedate camel, hitched to a railing which extended over the water trough there on the street, began to look angrily at the hecklers. Then, to enliven the party, some prankster goosed the camel with the end of a walking cane.

"AHNR-R-R-R!" the camel roared, and in the same instant it leaped. Its halter rope was strong, and the railing was torn loose. The beast swung its neck, which in turn swung the rope and the six-foot railing through the air as a truly lethal weapon. The massive club struck one A. H. Cooley squarely on the head, laying him so low that he was bedridden for a week. In the same motion, Joe Porterie's neck was skinned by the rope and his ear lobe torn and left dangling. Men began to shout and duck and run. The maddened camel had the whip hand, so to speak. It jumped right on the board sidewalk in front of the Bon Ton, upset chairs, broke a water cooler to bits, smashed a glass window, knocked down two posts so that the porch roof fell, backed into a buggy, and collapsed a wheel which in turn sent a team of buggy horses tearing down the street driverless. Then the camel swung back, upset the trough, and threw water all over Joe Porterie, who was now sprawled dazed in the dirt.

Only a miracle saved the town from a major disaster. That miracle appeared in the person of Hi Jolly himself. When Porterie had first come into Washington Street that evening, somebody sent for Hi at a local boardinghouse and told him one of his camels was in town. Hi came out to greet an old friend.

"Hey, calm down, my comrade!" Hadj Ali called in the Mohammedan dialect the camel understood. And it worked. The poor frightened animal recognized his master and came to a standstill in Miss Abbie McIntyre's beautiful bed of flowers. It subsequently cost Joe Porterie five dollars to appease Miss Abbie alone.

But during all this excitement, Joe had developed a respect for his camel—a sportsman's admiration for anything with spunk. "Hell, you can't blame the pore beast," Joe insisted. "It's you fool men that's to blame. Now who was it poked my camel with that cane?"

Fortunately, or perhaps unfortunately, there had been several witnesses. Mr. Horace Babcock, a well-to-do real-estate agent and gambler, was the man who had thought to have a little fun with his cane.

Without further ado, Joe Porterie went to Mr. Babcock and hung one on his chin. Babcock, his dignity wounded, reached for his pocket derringer, but Joe Porterie, whose ear was still bleeding, was all over him in two seconds. Thus the Bon Ton patrons and the town loafers had a double feature that evening. The next day an agreement was reached whereby Messrs. Porterie and Babcock split the bills and paid them. Both men had to wear bandages for a month.

Sunday was Sunday, and not to be profaned. Joe waited until Monday, then hired an Indian to "take this danged four-legged hoodoo out on the desert twenty miles or so and turn him loose. Here's a ten-dollar bill for your trouble."

The Indian agreed, and started leading the disdainful camel down a desert road. Joe congratulated himself. He even went to town to gloat with Hi Jolly over his vanishing troubles.

A little way beyond the present site of the state capital, however, the Indian met a farmer with a wagonload of hay drawn by a team of spirited horses. The horses saw and then scented the camel.

"Whoa-a-a-a!" the farmer howled. The horses ignored him. They tried to turn and run. The wagon was heavy and the road was narrow, but they got it around slantwise, then lunged, toppling it over into an irrigation ditch, with the hay underneath and the wagon wheels turning idly on top. The doubletree had broken off, and the horses went clattering away and eventually up the main streets of Phoenix.

The stolid Indian quite ignored the runaway horses, figuring that white man's business was none of his own. He led the camel four miles on down the road and met Lincoln Fowler, one of the wealthiest stockmen in Arizona Territory.

This day, Fowler was driving about two hundred fat hogs to market. Now hogs must be walked slowly, otherwise they lose valuable weight and may actually die from strain. They had been walking and grunting happily along, until the camel rounded a curve.

Whoof! Once more there was a stampede. Exactly as the cattle had done in Texas, the porkers fanned out to every point on the compass, except toward that weird hump-backed monster with the foreign smell. Mr. Fowler danced about in frenzy and frustration. About fifty of his finest hogs ran themselves into the hereafter, and others were still being hunted two days later.

Meanwhile, the hay that had toppled into the irrigation ditch had made a very effective dam. Water backed up, overflowed into a field and destroyed a valuable crop, pooled around a small adobe dwelling and melted it, and drowned nearly eighty of Mr. and Mrs. Bud Tasker's chickens.

One can guess who had to pay for all the damage. Joe didn't wait for Hi Jolly to deliver the walking jinx back to him this time. Hi was tending his rescued camel in a little desert lot. Joe went out there in the dead of night, slipped Hi some money, took the camel's lead rope, and personally led it—behind a docile old mare—far out toward Camelback Mountain. There Joe released the creature with his own hands. And with a profane blessing.

"I had figured to shoot the critter," Joe often told later. "It had cost me plenty, Lord knows. But I got to thinking.

It had been brought over here by white men in the first place. It hadn't done a thing wrong, of its own accord. Hell, I calculated it had a right to fight for a living, at least."

Other beasts of the original herd were getting into all sorts of scrapes as they roamed wild over the countryside. Men not acquainted with their history would come on one unexpectedly, shoot it dead, and investigate later. News of such killings all but broke Hi Jolly's heart. He was a kindly soul and couldn't understand the rough westerners, even after years of living among them. Not far from Camelback Mountain one day, Hi discovered some familiar tracks and followed them. He found five camels, one of which was newly born.

He had no trouble renewing the old friendship, although they had long been running wild. Without knowing exactly what he had in mind, he roped and led them back toward civilization. Perhaps he was impelled by some vague homesickness and yearning, and these beasts were his only link with his native land. At any rate, as he was leading them across the country some wandering cowboys saw him. They, too, were lonely and needed amusement. They began teasing Hi and finally forced him to make camp with them that evening.

When they wanted to slaughter one of the camels "to try out the taste of camel steak," Hi objected.

"You would not slaughter one of your horses for a steak," he pointed out.

"This here's different," a cowboy answered. "A camel ain't like a horse."

"My camels are not to be eaten," Hi Jolly ruled.

"Who says they ain't? And who are you, anyway? You're nothing but a daggoned A-rab. You ain't got no business in this country, anyway."

Hadj Ali was a man of intelligence and pride. He stood

up, took off the Arabian robe that he wore, flexed his muscles, and challenged: "I make it my business. I was hired to come here. I stay here. I mind my business, and you don't. Now I fight because you insult me."

That was excellent! A cowboy figures he can lick anybody else in the world, especially any foreigner. In about three minutes, though, the officious cowpuncher was prone on the ground, unconscious. Hi Jolly stood over him.

"Hell, you ain't goin' to git by with that!" a friend of the whipped cowboy cried.

But Hi got by with it. In turn, he laid out four men. Two remained. Then the inherent common sense of Americans again took charge, and one of these grinned: "Hell, Jolly, set down and have another cup'a coffee. You'd ought'a be tuckered some by now."

Presently the whole bunch was drinking coffee and eating a midnight snack together, and by morning the surly ones had got over their bad temper. Nobody ever molested Hi Jolly after that, and respect for him increased as the years passed.

But he released the camels and never again tried to corral them. They drifted over the wild lands and, one by one, were shot by hunters or pulled down by coyotes and cougars. One was captured and put in the zoo at Los Angeles. It died a few years ago, after seventy years of wondering at the strangeness of America. Its ashes were buried with those of Hadj Ali, under the monument that stands on an Arizona desert hill.

11

INSURRECTO!

SENSATION has always been heightened in the Southwest when Mexicans throw in a dash of their peculiar Latin spice. Given a handsome young revolutionist—a man at outs with the incumbent president—and a spunky as well as beautiful American girl, and we have the main ingredients for that altogether delightful something we call romance. Place the setting on a rancho in Mexico, and it is time to start the cameras turning!

A hero named Pico Tomás del Crespo y Flores and a heroine named Naomi Carr were the chief actors in this strange scenario, and theirs is a legend that could develop only in a country where people do unconventional things.

It began early one morning when a band of ragged men, opportunists in fact but *insurrectos* in fancy, charged yelling upon the Carr ranch in old Sonora and put it under siege.

Cavin Carr, adventurer and politician, defended the walled yard with his eighteen cowboys for half an hour, then waved a white napkin on a stick through the doorway.

"Why do you signal surrender?" his pretty young wife demanded. "We've got ammunition, food, water, everything we need."

"You let me handle it, Naomi," her husband answered. "That's Flores out there. I aim to get him."

"It was his ranch first. You took it from him, remember."

"The hell with that, now. If we fight here all day, some-body'll get hurt. I know a trick to match all his guns."

"A trick?" she planted herself before him, arms akimbo, her dark eyes flashing contempt. "You do everything that way."

"Mind your business!" Carr snapped. One thought stayed his opening the door. It was true they had supplies to stand off the siege indefinitely. You had to make a fortress of your home in Mexico in 1889, especially if you were a Yankee land-grabber. Wouldn't Flores and his peons, know-ing the defenders were amply provisioned, see through his deception?

It was a chance he would have to take, and Carr, a strange mixture of villain and hero, was capable of taking chances. He wrenched open the heavy door and strode out, hoisting high his flag of truce.

Naomi watched him, compelled to admire his courage. From windows and through rifle slits in the thick adobe his

loyal men squinted along their carbine barrels, lest any *insurrecto* fire upon their leader. The eighteen cowboys and the white-faced woman heard Carr call out for the enemy commander, Pico Tomás del Crespo y Flores.

The two captains met in a little arroyo in plain view of both forces. Naomi Carr's heart pounded as she awaited the treacherous shot from her husband's gun. In the ranch house fingers curved around triggers as the defenders made ready to cover Carr's retreat after he had killed Flores.

The parley between the two men continued for several breathless minutes. Then a peon stepped forward from the Mexicans' ranks carrying two swords. Naomi's heart leapt with pride. Cavin was not going to shoot his foe like a dog. He was going to fight an honorable duel.

The blades clashed furiously in the bright sunlight. One of the swordsmen went down. "My God!" croaked Bill Chastain, Carr's lieutenant. "That's the boss! Flores got him!"

An angry mutter arose. "Don't shoot," Mrs. Carr commanded. "I'm going out there. Tod and Alex, you come along."

"You aim to fetch the boss in, ma'am?"

"Yes." Her mouth was thin, her voice suddenly sharp. "And I'll bring my husband's killer in, too, sooner or later."

It was both promise and prophecy—a strange prophecy she was not aware of then.

Cavin Carr was dead when Naomi reached the arroyo. Flores stood silently, his sombrero in his hand, and a sparkle of admiration in his stare, as he watched the courageous beauty calmly direct the two cowboys to carry the corpse to the house. In a soft voice Flores apologized.

Mrs. Carr knew that the ranch had in effect been stolen from her husband's slayer and that he couldn't be blamed altogether for trying to regain his property. Nevertheless, she coldly informed Tomás Flores that he was under arrest.

He disagreed. "I go away now, *Señora*," he said, bowing. "I wait until you bury your hosban'. But I come back with *los insurrectos* to take my land. Is fair I warn you, *no es verdad?*"

He was downright gallant about it, but she whirled away before he finished and returned in fury to her warriors.

"Saddle your horses and ride those bandits down," she ordered. She could muster a force of possibly half the size of Flores' band, but her men were expert shots and eager to fight. She meant to hold the ranch. But by the time the avenging cavalcade thundered through the gate Flores and his band had withdrawn. Then began a chase which was to continue for five years to a surprising end.

Toward sunset the next evening, Chastain, who was leading the ranch force while Mrs. Carr remained behind to bury her husband, ran Flores into what seemed an inescapable trap. Most of the peons had joined the fiery Mexican for financial reward, and when hope of that failed they scattered. Flores found himself a "general" with an army of only a few more than a dozen men. When Chastain pushed close they and their leader took the first available refuge, in the ruins of a ranch house built a century or more before and abandoned about 1870 by one Jules Camou.

"Is water there, *amigos*," Flores told his loyal few, "and walls to protect us. Our horses can rest. Maybe so, in the night, we get another chance to flee."

Chastain ordered his men to surround the place. "We can starve them out," he said. "They won't have anything but water to live on."

Flores realized that he couldn't hold out. After nightfall he and a faithful lieutenant named Ocampo stole away. A wall of the Camou ranch house was crumbled at one corner. Dressed in dark clothing, the two men slithered over the ruins on their bellies. Random bullets whined through the night, but none touched the pair as they crawled some two hundred yards through Chastain's besieging fighters.

Dawn found Flores miles away. It also saw the surrender of the Mexicans who remained in the Camou fort. Chastain was angry and disappointed.

"The greaser can't be far," said he. "We'll pick up his trail."

But two days of searching brought no sign of the bandit leader. No peon would admit having seen him. Chastain decided to send his cowboy band back to the Carr rancho and continue the search alone. He made arrangements to receive messages from Mrs. Carr from time to time. It might be a long man hunt.

She sent him word to go after Flores by all means, and to encourage the pursuit offered a thousand-dollar reward in gold.

In seizing the rancho Cavin Carr had enjoyed the support of the Mexican government, and thus Flores was technically an outlaw. This meant that Chastain could call on officers whenever he felt like it, but it also meant that the impoverished peons were on Flores' side. He had often been their champion against oppression, and they would hide him.

Chastain rode up and down the rural districts asking for word of the hunted caballero.

"I have not see him, *Señor*," each farmer shrugged. "I go nowhere. Nobody come here."

Then one evening the American saw campfire smoke in a dry arroyo, far from any village or ranch. He rode over. From the top of the sandy embankment he looked upon a lone man hovering over a little fire. Chastain dismounted and slid down the steep bank.

"Who are you?" he demanded.

"Portes Ocampo," the man answered. "I herd the goats, *Señor*."

Chastain shot a quick glance around. There was no camp equipment of any kind. "Where is your tent, your duffel, and especially your goats?" he snapped.

Ocampo was trembling. His frightened glance darted up the embankment to where Chastain had left his horse. There was a quick tattoo of hoofbeats as the animal reared and then the steady drumming of a gallop as the mount was ridden away.

Chastain scrambled up the sandy bank and emptied both pistols toward the fading sound of hoofs, but he might as well have been shooting at a ghost. Too late he realized he had been a fool. The campfire was but a bait, and like a giddy moth he had gone right to it, while Flores lay hidden in the brush near by. Not only had the man-hunter lost his quarry, but now he was afoot and far from the nearest rancho.

One thing he could not understand. Surely by now Flores realized that Chastain was tracking him and meant to kill him. Why, then, had the outlaw let slip the golden opportunity to shoot his foe as he stood beside the campfire? What Chastain did not know was that Flores was not a killer at heart, nor even a bandit by choice. Circumstances had put him on the wrong side of the corral bars—that was all.

Chastain hoofed it back to the nearest village and reported his misadventure to Mrs. Carr. She sent him more money and two weeks later joined him at Cocorit, because it had been hinted that Flores was hiding out near the Sonora village.

Naomi Carr offered rich rewards for information about Flores, but there were no takers among the hungry peons. She wrote to the president of Mexico and received a flowery reply promising all possible assistance in running down her husband's killer, but this meant nothing. Mexico City was too far away for the government to bother about a ten-cent revolutionist in the hinterland. And after all, Carr had been only a gringo land-grabber.

Mrs. Carr's loyal lieutenant, Chastain, never ceased riding through the Sonora hills in search of his man. At last he remembered Ocampo, the trusted follower with whom Flores had escaped from the Camou ranch house and who had risked his own skin to help his master steal Chastain's horse. Through Ocampo there might be a way to Flores.

The wily man-hunter waited until Ocampo was absent from his small vegetable farm, and then approached the mistress of the domicile.

"*Señora,*" he said confidentially, as if guarding a secret, "I have news that you are the woman of Portes Ocampo, and I carry the message for him. It is a thing to be whispered."

A whispered secret for her man? What woman wouldn't be interested?

"*Que es, Señor?*" she murmured.

"Ah, but wait. It is for him direct. To be taken to one of importance. There is money, too."

If curiosity hadn't tempted her enough, the hint of money did. "Ocampo is not here today—not until tonight, *Señor.* Can I not carry the message for him? And the *pesos,* eh?"

Chastain turned on the mystery full blast. "But this is secret, I repeat. Do you, too, know the Señor Flores? He who is the friend of the people? He who was leader of a loyal army and was tricked?"

Her eyes said yes, though she remained silent.

"It is for him that I have the money, and a load of weapons, also. I was told to deliver these through Portes Ocampo, his loyal follower. But I have little time and if you . . ." He appeared to study the woman.

"Señor Flores is with *los insurrectos* at Santo Junipero!" she burst out. "Tomorrow they capture the train for the south. Portes goes with him. And I go with Portes!"

This was real news! "Then we are friends, in truth. Say nothing, my good woman. Here is some money. It is for you to keep. I will meet the train myself—if you say where."

"It is to be on the Great Slide, *Señor*. Where is the steep grade, and the narrow pass. If you tie a bit of red cloth on your arm—I will give you such a piece."

Thus did Chastain himself join the *insurrecto* movement, actually donning their red identification badge. He tried to pose as a Mexican, because he was very tanned and he spoke the language well. He thought thus to locate Tomás Flores and either kill him or deliver him to federal officers for trial.

Because recruits were welcome it was easy for Chastain to join the *insurrecto* band, but a superior officer quickly recognized him for what he was.

"You are gringo, eh?" the officer said. "All right, you fight with us if you wish, but see you do not make the trouble." His warning was clear, and Chastain could do nothing that day but crouch in hiding, awaiting the train raid.

He first saw Flores after the train had been stopped. While rifles were cracking at the engine crew and men were scrambling down to capture the prize, Flores appeared, climbing up the caboose steps. Chastain acted with American rashness.

"You, Flores!" he shouted.

It was not a thing for a peon private to do. Officers and men looked questioningly at him.

Flores had heard. He saw Chastain not fifty feet away pointing a rifle at him. Instantly he lifted his pistol and fired.

The bullet missed. Chastain's rifle cracked. He missed, too. Flores ran up the steps and across the back platform and leaped off the other side. He rolled down the roadbed embankment and fled.

Chastain pursued as rapidly as possible, but when he reached the other side of the caboose, his man was diving into some brush for cover. The cowboy snapped another shot. Flores whirled and fired quickly once more. Chastain dropped his gun and clapped both hands to his side. He staggered a few feet, then fell.

As for the other Mexicans, they accepted this sideshow drama as a part of the main battle. The train was captured and the army loaded on it, the wounded included. That night Chastain came to his senses many miles to the south. He was in great pain and badly wounded. For nearly three months he was unable to report to Mrs. Naomi Carr that he had caught up with his man but had failed to capture him.

Nothing more was heard of Flores for almost a year. The management of the big rancho took all of Naomi Carr's time, and its security no longer seemed threatened with attack by the former owner. She lost much of her zest for his blood.

Chastain, however, was far from ready to give up the man hunt. Three times he had been bested by the handsome outlaw, and the wound in his side still twinged with each change of the weather. Thirsting for vengeance, he clung to his enemy's trail.

Eventually he learned that Flores' family owned an old mining property in the state of Guanajuato, five hundred miles to the south. Doggedly the cowboy turned his horse toward central Mexico.

It took him four months to ferret out the information that Flores possessed a mine there and that recently the claim had begun to pay rich dividends, after having lain idle for years. Did this mean that the outlaw himself had reopened the property? Chastain believed so.

Within another month he had learned that attorneys Menche and Trevino in the little capital city of Guanajuato were handling the mine's business. And then a police official there told Chastain that Tomás Flores himself was around the town. He was no longer in danger of arrest; the government had changed, and his party was in power. The cowpoke from the north visited the lawyers, posing as a friend of their young client.

"You are fortunate, *Señor*," Alvaro Menche said. "Flores comes to this office every day. Will you wait for him here?"

"No, outside. I have ridden far and am thirsty. There is a *cantina* next door from where I can see Tomás approach."

He paused in the doorway of the building to scan the passers-by on the sidewalk. Coming toward him, scarcely thirty feet away, was Tomás Flores!

The Mexican spied the cowboy at the same instant. He stopped in his tracks, unable to believe his eyes. Chastain moved forward, his hand dropping to his belted gun. Flores spun and raced away.

In recounting the adventure years later, Flores said that at each step he expected a bullet in the back. But the sidewalk was crowded and Chastain held his fire lest he kill an innocent person. He meant to chase his prey into the open where Tomás could be dispatched with ease.

Flores, however, knew the town, and his pursuer did not. They sped through crooked alleys, the Mexican always able to keep a corner between himself and Chastain's gun. Finally the American came to a plaza opening on the city's cemetery. Flores was nowhere in sight. The cowboy shrugged and gave up the chase.

In the nick of time Tomás Flores had found sanctuary among the dead, scrambling into a vacant vault built into the cemetery wall in European fashion. That night he slipped out to the railroad yards and boarded a train for Mexico City still farther south. Where, he wondered as the wheels clacked over the rails, could he hide from the gringo's relentless search?

For a time Chastain sulked in Guanajuato. "If I had shot him on the streets here," he wrote Mrs. Carr, "I would have been arrested and likely sent to prison. So I tried to chase him—and I lost him."

Mrs. Carr wanted to call off the human bloodhound. "Let the past die of itself, and come on back home," she urged. "There is no need of carrying this thing forever."

But Chastain still was not ready to give up. He believed that Flores would come back to collect his mine profits sooner or later; so he hung around Guanajuato for months, even calling on the attorneys again. The lawyers confessed they had lost touch with their client completely and were very much disturbed about it.

No one today knows exactly why Chastain went south to Mexico City instead of returning to Sonora. It seems unlikely that he had definite news of the man he was trailing, for this time Flores had effectively cloaked his identity.

But journey to the capital the American did. And although he was not a devotee of the sport, he attended a bullfight. He was not greatly interested in the excitement in the ring below. Instead, his eyes roamed restlessly among the cheering spectators, seeking out certain familiar chiseled features.

He did not find them in the stands, but when the carcass of the last bull was being hauled from the arena to be butchered for the poor, Chastain recognized the ragged driver of the mule which towed the dead beast away. Tortured by the fear of being hunted, Tomás Flores had taken a mean job in the bull ring, hoping no one who knew him would spot him there.

Chastain pushed his way through the departing throng and skirted the stands to the back lot where nearly one hundred beggars waited for the bull to be cut up and parceled out. A corporal's guard of armed police was keeping order among the clamoring crowd. The American rushed up with his revolver in his hand. "All right you murdering—! This time I'm going to kill you!"

Flores was unarmed except for his long mule whip. Chastain fired, risking arrest in Mexico rather than his hated foe's escape.

Flores leaped aside as the gun barked. Chastain's bullet went wide and killed an innocent boy in the crowd. Angry shouts arose. Flores swung the mule whip. It cracked like a pistol and jerked the American's gun arm. Like a striking snake, the coil of the whip lashed out again, cutting Chastain in the face and blinding him. Then came the report of another gun!

It was a Mexican policeman who fired. Chastain was his target. The officer knew nothing of the cause of the American's attack. He saw only that a boy was already dead and other innocent bystanders were in panic. So he shot the crazy gringo—shot him dead!

That was the policeman's explanation in police court. It made sense to the magistrate and jury. The officer was exonerated and even complimented for his prompt action. Flores, the poor muleteer, was congratulated for his bravery with the whip.

Dazed, and yet elated with the knowledge that he was a free man at last, Flores left the courtroom and walked for six hours before he regained his normal senses. Then he caught a freight and rode the rods back to Guanajuato.

"Tomás, *amigo!*" his attorney greeted him. "Where in the name of heaven have you been? There is much property for you, much wealth from the mine. Why do you simply disappear for a year or more at a time, you young rascal?" It was a heartwarming welcome. Pico Tomás del Crespo y Flores broke down in tears.

The long game of cat and mouse was over, but the story

was not. Tomás Flores stayed in Guanajuato and piled up considerable wealth from his mines. He was still reasonably young, although a hard life had given him a seriousness of mien and manner somewhat beyond his years. He lived simply, almost frugally. One day he asked his attorneys' aid in getting a money order for a sum equivalent to fifty thousand dollars in American money.

"What is this for, Tomás?" Menche asked.

"I wish it made payable to Señora Naomi Carr," he said. "It will be restitution, in part, for the harm I did her."

"Harm you did? But it was her husband who stole your rancho in the beginning! From your father's estate! The land that should have been your own!"

"I wish to send her the money."

The draft was duly mailed. Within the month came the widow's acknowledgment:

"I cannot think what to say to you, Señor Flores. The kindness of your letter, plus the money, leaves me with a feeling of shame. I am well aware that Cavin Carr preempted land which was yours by right, and that so-called politics did not make this honest. I do not defend him, and I have not mourned him, although I did try to avenge him for a time. I can respect you for trying to take by force what was originally yours. Your money, therefore, I cannot accept, because it is not owed to me, and I bear you no ill will. I therefore return it to you herewith."

Flores' sense of guilt in having his money returned died quickly in his elation over her admission that Naomi Carr had forgiven him. He showed the letter to Menche with voluble joy.

"She is a beautiful woman, *amigo*," he praised. "Even when she stood beside her husband's body, hating me like a rattlesnake, I saw only that she was lovely. But why does she send back the money?"

"Perhaps she does not need it. Or maybe it is pride."

"Pride. Ah, that it is, pride!"

The wise lawyer studied his friend several minutes, then took him by the arm. "Tomás, go pack a bag for travel. We shall call on the Señora Carr."

"My friend!" Flores cried. "You are truly my friend!"

By rail, stage, and horse they went to the Carr rancho, arriving there on October 6, 1894. After the servants took charge of the guests' mounts, Señora Carr herself appeared on the wide front porch.

She was dressed in blue. She was then about thirty years of age, but she was small of stature and looked much younger. She was quiet-mannered, and she was still beautiful.

"You are welcome, gentlemen," she said simply. "Señor Flores, I never live in the past; I do not even think of it. You both must be weary from travel. Please come in and rest before dinner."

This was the second meeting between Naomi Carr and Tomás Flores. The overtone of formality continued for perhaps forty-eight hours. Then by degrees, under Menche's tactful guidance, a more delightful intimacy began to bloom.

Menche was a shrewd friend as well as a brilliant attorney. He pretended a deep interest in the geology of the countryside as an excuse for staying on longer than "business discussions" might have made necessary. And this gave the necessary time for other matters to develop. One day Naomi and Tomás came to him, smiling broadly.

"Alvaro," Flores said, "you must make arrangements for my wedding."

Naomi Carr, as the Señora Flores, lived until 1923, in a happiness completely unclouded by the past. And Tomás Flores, a man of many years and much dignity, still lives at this writing with relatives deep in Mexico, cherishing memories as strange as the picturesque land of his youth.

12

BROKEN ARROW

In this beautiful autumn of 1871, no one could have convinced little Wassaja that the world wasn't perfect, peaceful, serene, and likely to remain so forever. His days were as happy as those of a savage child could be. He was one of three hundred Apache Indians, the fiercest warriors in the wilderness, who had been encamped for almost a month on Iron Mountain. At age six, Wassaja had no important duties.

"Go and catch mice," his black-skinned mother ordered, "or play in the icy stream."

She wanted him out from under foot—as what mother doesn't when she is busy?—and she pointed to the crimson maples on the mountaintop above and to the golden carpet made by leaves of the quaking aspen. This was the paleface month of October, if Wassaja had but known it. But Wassaja had never seen a white person, nor had any of the Apaches in the camp, except some of the older warriors. That any person could be white of skin—actually white, as if bleached out by the drainage of blood and strength—was beyond his comprehension. He and his little friends sometimes spoke of it, as they would speak of thunder gods and lightning devils and such comparable phenomena; but on the whole they were not much interested. The realities of day-to-day living were sufficiently absorbing.

"If you do not stay around all the time," mother promised

178

one day, "I will see to it that you get to lick the scrapings."

The scrapings? It might have been a mother of today promising a child he might lick a cake pan. But this mother of the wilderness, named Thil-ge-ya, like other women of the camp was baking mescal. This was why the Apaches had encamped here on the mid-altitude slope of the mountain. Picturesque century plants—mescal, the Spaniards called them, or agave—dotted the countryside like fantastic sentinels, their giant flower stalks often reaching up twenty, thirty, and even forty feet. Around them among the rocks were hundreds of the beautiful leaf rosettes, growing plants which were readying themselves to blossom any time within ten to seventy years. It was these leaves that attracted the Indians. They might be harvested, chopped into pieces, baked in a pit of hot rocks for twenty-four hours, then converted into highly nutritious food. The mescal came from the pit resembling a mixture of molasses and straw, and was spread on the smooth side of deerskins to be kneaded and allowed to harden into cakes like slabs of bacon. To scrape the sweet candy-like leavings, then, was a childhood joy in Apache-land.

The men of the camp were hunting, drinking tiswin (an Apache firewater), and loafing. They were inordinately arrogant and proud. For more years than he had lived, little Wassaja knew, these men had raided lesser Indians, the Pimas especially, soft and fearful farmers who lived in the valleys. Apache men would swoop down in late autumn, steal the Pimas' harvests of corn, squash and beans, kidnap their comeliest women, and return to the wild free hills. These sallies were great adventures, even for the youngsters of the Apache band who were allowed to share in the loot and watch the torturing of captives. No Pima group had ever won a battle with the Apaches. Pimas, of all enemies, were to be held in contempt.

But fate had prepared a strange hand of cards to deal little Wassaja that fall. In his inherited contempt for the Pimas, he did not know how they craved vengeance. He could not have known which of the gods, if any, directed two young Pima men to go exploring in the direction of Iron Mountain that same golden month of October. But go they did, and they dared venture far beyond the line of safety.

"If we push on up into the hills," one said to the other, "we may come onto a fine buck. It would be a trophy to take back to the Pima chieftain."

It would, indeed, for the Pimas usually had too little meat. The two men, grown boys really, moved farther and farther into the Apache territory, but they moved warily, ever alert. They would go across this valley, over this rise, up this canyon, along this ridge, being careful to stay screened, but adventuring always. The third night out they were walking a narrow canyon that seemed to have high walls and extend for miles up towards the distant clouds. Suddenly one of them stopped motionless, signaling to his companion.

"Smell!" he whispered.

They sniffed the air. An unmistakable odor of baking mescal came down the canyon! During the day, hot air from the lower altitudes cause up-currents in such places, but by night the currents reverse, and the presence of Apaches was instantly detected.

"Are you—afraid?" one asked.

It was a challenge, and both knew it. The other smiled. Old friends, they knew what they longed to do, and they agreed to do it. They crept on up the canyon instead of fleeing; they went by night and scouted the Apache camp where little Wassaja lived. In time, they crept back and reported to their Pima chieftain.

Four dawns later, while the Apache camp was still somnolent in arrogance and pride, with not even a sentinel out, fate dealt the first of her cards destined to change the entire life of little Wassaja.

Pima warriors had come by the hundreds and crept all around the camp of the Apaches. Each Pima carried a little pot of live coals and some dried grass twisted for making torches quickly. They edged up like shadows, closer, closer, an inch at a time. At the right moment the chief gave a signal—a coyote's cry. Demons with firebrands then appeared as if from nowhere and raced to the wickiups of the Apaches. The wickiups themselves were made of thatched reeds and straw—tinder ready for igniting. In a matter of seconds, the thatch of every wickiup home was burning.

No Apache had been awake. Now one squaw came to life and darted to the door of her wickiup. *Zip!* The Pima arrow passed through her breast. A man appeared in another door: a spear came from the flame-lit night and pierced his bowels.

"Wah-wah-wah-wah-wah-ee-yah-WA-A-A-AH!"

No man has known supreme terror until he has been awakened by the war cry of the American Indian. Among all tribes it had a similarity. Here on Iron Mountain it was a mockery, for the Pimas used the intonations of the Apaches themselves. More Apache men crawled out of their homes, to die in the instant. Still more were trapped in the crackling flames. A mother came out holding a baby, and at once a Pima warrior darted to them on horseback; he tomahawked the mother and tossed her and her babe into the flames of their own home. Screams echoed from the high cliffs near the camp and mingled with the derisive laughter of the Pima braves. After long years of defeat and suffering, the Pimas were making one swift thrust of revenge.

From this hell of death and danger ran a little boy of six

years, naked as sin, plump like a butternut, and fully as brown. Wassaja had no plan, no real knowledge of what was happening; he was just frightened beyond words or thoughts at all, and so he just intuitively ran.

Another Pima horseman darted from the ring of attackers. Wassaja had never seen a horse before. Here, in the eerie light of the burning dwellings, he saw his first horse carrying a rider and thought the two were the same animal, somehow connected. Moreover, the hideously frightening beast dashed right toward him, snorting wildly from one head, yelling fiendishly from another. Before he could think further, Wassaja felt a hand reach down and grab him by the hair. The next instant he was up on top of the horse, riding before the manlike portion of it. Then, praise God, blessed oblivion came to the little boy. He saw no more of the massacre. He did not know for years that of the three hundred Apaches, only a scant dozen survived that dawn raid by the Pimas.

He regained his senses while riding with the triumphant warriors back to the Pima village, miles away. And in their village, he was tortured mildly for days. His captor would not let him be seriously injured, for the man planned to sell the boy as a slave. But the squaws and the other children in the Pima camp were permitted to "enjoy" Wassaja.

It was considered high fun to throw him to the ground and urinate on him. It was even more fun to brandish sharp axes at him, to put red ants on him, to jab his buttocks with saguaro cactus thorns. These were all tricks practiced by the Apaches themselves on their captives, as the Pimas had excellent reason to know. Hence they now had no compunction. But the time came when the Pimas wearied of such entertainment, and one day Wassaja's captor put him on another horse, took him to the white man's village of Florence, Arizona, and offered him for sale.

Now, who would want to buy a savage Indian child? Who, especially, would want a little Apache boy, too small to be of any help as a worker, too wild in background to be accepted into any family group that termed itself civilized? However much of human feelings our earlier settlers may have had, it must be remembered that Apaches were regarded as something less than human.

"Give me six horses for him," the Pima brave demanded.

White folk gathered around, but made no offers. The Pimas were friends of the whites; there had been no warfare between them. But this offer was a suggestion of slavery, which had already been condemned in our nation. So the offer became entertainment only. Little Wassaja could only stare in bewilderment and fear. Life had been much too swift for him lately.

"Two horses and a bottle of whiskey," the Pima brave asked, next.

Still there were no buyers. And still more and more

white men and women came just to stare in mixed emotions at a little captive Apache boy. Finally, in God's mercy, an itinerant photographer drove down the street of Florence. He was Carlos Gentilé (pronounced "Jen-Til'-ly") a native Italian educated in the United States. He had a wagon pulled by mules, in which he carried equipment for taking the tintypes of the period. "Whoa," said he, reining up when he saw little brown Wassaja standing naked there.

The onlookers told him what was happening, and several men grinned. "Whyn't *you* buy him yoreself, Gentilé?" one asked. "You're a bachelor, with no family of yore own."

Mr. Gentilé climbed down from his wagon seat. He was trembling a little with emotion, even as Wassaja trembled in cold and fear.

"I have just thirty silver dollars," the photographer said. "I will pay that for him."

The Pima brave squinted at the sun, which was now sinking low. He glared at the whites, who grinned back at him. Finally he held out his hands, and Gentilé clinked the thirty coins into them, one at a time, and without another word took the frightened little boy by the hand and led him to his living quarters in a wooden studio-home near by. He led him inside a room—the first room in the first white home the lad had ever entered—and left him there to go care for the wagon and team.

Alone in this strange place, Wassaja immediately discovered that he was *not* alone. Paleface magic struck him with full force, for lo—on the walls of the room were dozens of little people no taller than his hand! Some were sitting, some were standing, some appeared to have no legs or torsos. All were miniature, and all stared at him with a steady seriousness. Then he realized that these people were staring at him from dark little windows in the wall, and he began to move around the room to see them better and perhaps to

184

catch a glimpse of the outdoors, too. But not one of them moved; they just stared fixedly, until he came to a larger and brighter window. There, astonishingly, he suddenly beheld another Apache boy his own age and size! Indeed, if he had not been so bewildered, he would have thought this second boy precisely like his own image which he had seen in still pools of streams, in the days before the massacre.

"Where am I? Will you help me?" he murmured to the other little boy.

The other one spoke back, but silently. Wassaja leaned to catch his whisper, and he leaned too but did not whisper. As Wassaja moved, the other boy moved. So perfect and persistent was this mimicry that Wassaja soon found himself sobbing uncontrollably; hysteria had set in.

He spent all that first night and the next day trying to fathom the white man's mysteries: the photographs, the mirror, the clock, the clothing, the furniture, the food. Mr. Gentilé came for him next morning, lifted him tenderly from an incredibly soft and therefore uncomfortable bed— a far cry from his own accustomed bed of skins on the ground of the wickiup—then spoke to him as father to son.

"You must call me, boy," the man purred gently. "Don't just wet things when you want to go. Either get up yourself and go outside, or call your papa. I'm your papa now, eh? I expect you don't know a word I say, but you will, you will, eh? We'll git you some britches today, yessiree, and learn you plenty of things."

By ten o'clock he was prepared to bathe his little ward, and because the interest among his neighbors was so great, he decided to do it outside in the town square, near the public well. There he brought a wooden tub, filled it with water, and stripped Wassaja. Dozens of spectators came, all with friendly intent. Lather more copious than that of the amole root which Wassaja had known at home was worked from some magic again, and the boy covered with it. Rags, even brushes, were used to scrub him. Wassaja felt that he understood this completely; he was being washed so that his black color would go away and he would be a paleface in fact as well as in adoption; he would be like the white man who now "owned" him. And when his new clothes were donned, and he looked down at his skin to find it as dark as ever, he burst into sobbing once more. It was not fear this time, as people said; it was disappointment.

The next step was to take Wassaja to the town priest. There Mr. Gentilé and the Reverend A. Eschallier conferred, and the good father offered a suggestion.

"It would not do to give a black son your name in full," said he. "But the name 'Carlos' might be given."

"I would be pleased," Mr. Gentilé confessed.

"Well, for a surname—one recalls that the great patron saint of all aborigines in the Southwest from down in Mexico was Montezuma. A heathen, to be sure, but a powerful one. It would be apt to name your son of the wilderness for that man."

Carlos Gentilé nodded, and so then and there little Wassaja, born in a wickiup on a mountain side, a child of the forest and of the rocky deserts, was named in the Christian way and became Carlos Montezuma.

The last thing the Italian-born Gentilé said to the priest was, "I am proud of him, father. I will now leave this frontier and take him to civilization. I will not allow my son to be reared in ignorance, I will give him the best education a modern boy can have."

It is regrettable that space does not permit a detailed account of young Carlos' reincarnation, of his transformation into a white boy in every detail except color of skin. Indeed, it is regrettable that we cannot record here the steps in which he learned to eat, drink, and speak in paleface fashion. For we have all those details and more. But the saga of Carlos Montezuma moves now into urban America, at least for a while.

Young Carlos Montezuma was graduated *cum laude* from the University of Illinois just thirteen years after he saw his first white man! With a bachelor of science degree he entered Chicago Medical College on June 21, 1884. He worked in a drugstore to help pay his expenses, and he was further aided by the Urbana Young Men's Christian Association. And what of Gentilé, his guardian? We know that a loving Gentilé guided and protected him for years as they traveled up and down the Atlantic seaboard, schooled him in New York City and Chicago, and enjoyed his companionship in Carlos' boyhood years in a fine photographic salon in Chicago at 3907 Cottage Grove Avenue, "Horses and Carriages Photographed as a Specialty." We know that Gentilé's portrait hung for years in the Chicago Press Club and that he now lies buried in the Press Club cemetery. But that's all. No research, no available records show much more information about the man or why he and his adopted son were estranged.

In medical school a great new enthusiasm came to Carlos Montezuma. "If I have done this well," said he, "if I who was a savage Apache Indian have proved my worth in the white man's world, then I am proof that all Indians could do so. Plainly, all that the red man needs is a chance."

This attitude was not conceit with him but discovery. The red brain was as good, potentially, as the white. Thus Montezuma became a crusader, a man who exercised his very forceful personality, his keen wit in oratory, and his biting trenchant pen and began thumping the nation in a campaign of reform for the American Indian. Even before he won his medical degree this conviction had become a

187

passion with him. He was already famous when he took his first job, as physician in a Dakota Indian agency, because of his fearless attacks on the United States Indian Bureau. He pointed a pitiless finger at the incompetency, the floundering, and the widespread graft. He set out a specific program of reform, one that would permit the Indian himself—and not the white employee of the bureau—to receive the benefit from moneys appropriated. He showed the way toward a sensible program of education, which would retain the best of native culture and push the red man only part way up the paleface road and aim at the Indian's social as well as economic advancement. It was, in truth, the most comprehensive, most humanitarian—and most revolutionary—program ever advocated for the American Indian.

Needing more money to further this philanthropic campaign, and being at outs with Uncle Sam anyway, now, Dr. Montezuma left the government service and formed a partnership with the distinguished Dr. Fenton B. Turck in Chicago. This partnership prospered. Montezuma, far from being an Indian mystic or "medicine man," was a distinguished (and distinguished-looking) physician by all standards. Highly cultured for his day, he was sought after by the elite of society. He became wealthy in a few years. He did much charity practice. Though christened a Catholic, he joined the Baptist church, then became a Master Mason and Knight Templar. He married a beautiful Hungarian woman, Maria Keller, after a boy-meets-girl romance. He owned a big home and drove around Chicago in fine carriages with rubber tires. And then with his hard-earned money he set out more avidly than ever to campaign for Indian reform.

Besides distributing at his own expense millions of leaflets and pamphlets written by himself, he went on several lecture tours to major cities and universities. Everywhere he found the whites sympathetic, but also apathetic—exactly as they had been before. At last in desperation Dr. Montezuma decided to go to the Indians themselves.

Traveling to Phoenix, Arizona, and from there back to his own homeland (a touching chapter in his broader biography), he tried through an interpreter to arouse the Apaches, who lived in squalor even though warfare had ended.

"I am one of you!" he orated, in passionate zeal. "Look at me! What I have done, any Apache can do. Arise! Demand your rights! Help me to get what is appropriated for you. Help me to help yourselves!"

And did they follow this Messiah? As at Jesus himself, the people scoffed—the Apaches, and the Pimas, and the Navahos, and the Hopis—all with whom he pleaded.

"He is a fool," these red men decided. "He has plenty to eat, plenty to wear, and a roof over his head. What more can a man want? What does he worry about us for? He is Dr. Tom-Tom, drumming for nothing. He is a broken arrow that has shot itself against a rock cliff."

These people could not understand the missionary instinct—that one significant difference between savagery and civilization. They laughed at him and derided him, even when he tried valiantly to get himself reinstated as a member of the Apache tribe. Back in Washington—as one can well imagine—the paleface politicians laughed in their own triumphant way. Only one really great Washingtonian tried to back him; Theodore Roosevelt called him to the White House and offered him a job as head of the Indian Bureau itself! But then fate took a slap at Carlos Montezuma; he became suddenly ill. Back in Chicago with his wife, he languished a few days, then called her to his side.

"Maria," said he, "you must close out my business, collect all the bills you can, then follow me. I am going to Arizona, to stay."

He said no more, offered no explanation. His wife suspected that his illness was tuberculosis, which it was. But in one short week he had become uncommunicative, refusing to see patients or friends, refusing even to talk more with Maria. She saw him take the train alone. Already his hundred-and-eighty-pound frame was wasting.

In Phoenix, he hired a carriage and had himself driven many miles from any human habitation, far up near old abandoned Fort McDowell, where the wild Apaches once roamed. He built a wickiup of reeds and limbs exactly as his ancestors had done. Then he stripped off all his clothing, wrapped himself in a single blanket and lay down on the cold December ground to die.

By sheer chance, Dr. C. H. Ellis, a medical missionary to the Arizona Indians, heard of the "strange hermit" far off in a lone wickiup and dutifully rode up there. He found a mere shadow of a once large man, a sufferer who had a little food and a vessel of water, but absolutely nothing else. For an hour the dying one refused to talk. Then Dr. Ellis saw a Masonic ring.

"Why I'm a Mason, too," Ellis said. "Tell me, what is your name?"

"Montezuma," the emaciated fellow murmured.

Dr. Ellis was appalled. "Are you—*Doctor* Montezuma? My God, I see that you are!"

"Get out!" the sick man raved. "Don't touch me! Go away and let me die! I don't want you here!"

Maria Keller Montezuma was telegraphed, and she came at once. Her husband, who had always loved her tenderly, tried now to drive her out of his wickiup. She could not help him in any way, nor could any one else; he had become a ferocious, pitiful, half-human thing. Still in his blanket, he died during a rainstorm on January 31, 1923. Burial was on the desert there a few days later, and when the white ceremony was done, a troup of Indian women came forward and began to chant. Over the grave it was not a death chant, but a paean of victory, a mystical service beyond the white people's ken.

Perhaps, in some measure, those Indian women understood his failure, his frustration in trying to serve his fellows, and foresaw his victory in a day to come. For the advances in Indian service reforms going forward today are largely those propounded years ago by Dr. Carlos Montezuma, alias Dr. Tom-Tom, the Broken Arrow.[1]

[1] For a complete book-length biography of Carlos Montezuma, see the author's *Savage Son* (Albuquerque, University of New Mexico Press, 1951), from which this story, greatly condensed, is taken.

13

JAILBIRDS OF THE OLD SOUTHWEST

THE CATTLE BARON felt absolutely certain that the cards of politics were stacked against him. He faced a felony charge, and even the judge was his enemy. The trial date was still four months away, but he went to the judge immediately and did an amazing thing.

The following week he rode—proudly on his finest horse —two hundred miles to the territorial prison and presented an official paper to the warden.

"H-m-m-m-m!" the warden grunted, reading. "You say you are the prisoner yourself! No officer with you? And no—no conviction?"

"I bring my own commitment papers," the rancher asserted. "Special favor of the judge. The least sentence I can hope for is twelve months. This is slack season on the ranch now, but I expect to be exceedingly busy next year, so I asked the judge to let me start serving my sentence in advance."

"I never heard tell of such!"

However, the paper was legal, and the warden let him in. An hour later the rancher was wearing stripes.

For nearly four months he lived with the most notorious collection of criminals the Wild West ever knew; he labored and slept and suffered and even fought with them. But when his trial was held back home with the defendant *in absentia*, the jury found him not guilty! Therefore, when he received the news, the prisoner removed his stripes, shook hands with the warden, and rode away on his fine horse.

That Territorial Prison at Yuma, Arizona, has taken on stature over the decades as the most picturesque, most interesting jail not only in the Southwest but in the entire nation. It was like a scene from the motion picture *Beau Geste* (which, incidentally, was filmed near by). It was a thing for fiction, yet the stark reality of it was more impressive than any fiction could be. It was carved out of a granite mountain in the hottest spot imaginable—the sun is almost killing in its intensity on that desert plain—in the year 1876, and until 1909 bedeviled and bedamned men from the entire Mexican frontier country were imprisoned in this hell hole.

Escape was "impossible." Hard, heavy tools, drills, and dynamite or powder were necessary to cut through the granite walls of the cells, authorities said. Doors were made of bars of iron heavier than any used on a jail theretofore. Guards with rifles patrolled every wall, and a Gatling gun was ready night and day in a special water-tank tower commanding the yards. Suppose, though, a man did get out over or through the outer wall. On one side, the treacherous Colorado River faced him, and its eddies have taken many a man to his doom. Beyond that and all around on every side lay two hundred miles of waterless desert, much of it sand unrelieved by vegetation. Across and beyond the two hundred miles Indians waited to scalp the escaped convict or bring him back for a fat reward. Yet such a formidable place is always a challenge to desperate men, many of whom develop a courage beyond all reason. Their stories make Yuma jail an everlasting part of the sun-country legend.

Among the best tales (all may be found in official records) is that of the "four good men." These four convicts did no fighting and plotted no bloodshed. Life-termers, they elected to serve their sentence peacefully and hope. They bunked together in the same tiny cell. They won considerable respect. But one August the 110-degree temperature—the standard summer range around Yuma—got the better of them, and they planned an escape.

Five years later they were ready! All that time they had worked on their plan. Each night they had dug on a secret tunnel extending from the bottom of their cell to a point outside the prison wall. For tools they used spoons, nails, and broken bottles. Dirt and rock chips they smuggled out in the cuffs of their trousers and in their hatbands. A rag rug covered the tunnel entrance. One night they measured the length of the tunnel and discovered they were almost ready for flight. Sure enough, a last poke or two revealed a crack of liberty's light! However, this was at dawn. Escape by day would be doubly hard; they could wait fifteen more hours. But through the day their elation swelled.

At breakfast all four were hilarious. During their morning work they showed constant animation. And by recreation time one of them laughed and danced crazily in anticipation, a victim of his own emotions. A squint-eyed guard eyed him and drawled, "Damned if you jays ain't been acting fools all day. I'll just have a look around yore cell."

Two of the four eventually died in prison, and the other two served almost thirty years each.

How they would have traversed the desert sands outside is still a matter for speculation, but the manner in which two other prisoners did so is known. These two were incorrigibles who had worn heavy iron chains and balls for more than ten years. They were laboring outside the prison wall on day near the railroad and paused to gaze longingly at a locomotive wheezing near by. That engine was a symbol of everything for which they yearned.

"Say, look!" one prisoner suddenly whispered. "Nobody's in that engine. And it's got up steam!"

His companion stared.

"Nobody's in sight and I can run a train!" the first one went on, stooping to lift his irons. "Plenty of files and such in an engine tool box to cut these things off our legs! Come on!"

Before any guard saw them they were puffing away! The chuff-chuff-chuff was a staccato of freedom, and these two convicts sang as they cut off their heavy balls and chains. In half an hour they were loose for the first time in a decade. If they could just ride across the worst of the desert, escape was certain.

Then, tragically, the locomotive stopped. It was out of water, and no more was to be had.

"It's all right!" one man cried. "It's only four or five miles yonder to the mountains now. We can find drinking water there. They'll never catch us!"

But when the two started to run on foot, they stumbled and fell. They tried again and fell, then again and again. They could not run nor even walk with ease; ten years in heavy irons had nearly crippled them. They had progressed less than two miles when the posse caught them.

Thomas Gates was warden of Yuma Prison for several years. One morning, as Tom entered the front gate, he was instantly seized by prisoners. His arrival had been a signal! Using Tom as a shield, they would escape. But one guard, a crack shot named Hartlee, shouted down from his cubbyhole on top of the west wall.

"I can clip buttons off you men and never hurt one of you! You got ten seconds to turn Tom loose!"

They ignored him, and Hartlee began firing rapidly. The prisoners tried to squat behind the warden as they had planned. But Hartlee needed only a glimpse of a head, a shoulder, a hip, or a knee for a target. He dropped men all around Tom Gates. In desperation one prisoner then drew a knife and stabbed Tom in the back. The prisoner was shot to death and the riot stopped.

Mr. Gates died years after Yuma Prison was abandoned, and as old age settled on him sentiment was given full play. He loved to tell about that episode, and to an attentive listener he would present the "very knife" with which he had been stabbed. Fond friends said after his funeral that Tom had given away at least twenty such knives.

"Mother" F. S. Ingalls was the beloved wife of another warden who served many years at Yuma. For a long time she supplied that touch of gentleness which transformed the place from an earthly hell to a bearable abode. She sewed on buttons, comforted the sick, and mended hearts in many,

many ways, and most of the prisoners loved her with a fierce respect.

One morning Mother Ingalls was kneading biscuit dough when a premeditated prison break began. On signal, guards were overpowered, and a concerted rush was made for the main gate. In the same moment a smuggled rifle was used to kill the guard in the Gatling-gun tower. Mother saw it all from her kitchen window. Distressed, she suddenly ran across the compound.

Before the prisoners could realize it, the Gatling was barking death again. It was an old four-barrelled forerunner of the modern machine gun. Mother Ingalls herself was turning the crank.

"What'll we do!" the frantic prisoners yelled at their leaders.

"Shoot her down, you fools! This ain't a time to be chicken-hearted!"

The man with the smuggled rifle lifted it to fire. Mother Ingalls flattened him. Somebody else seized the rifle and emptied it at her, but she won the battle singlehanded. Surgeons worked all day mending wounded men, but within an hour Mother was back at her biscuit dough.

Jack Swilling was less fortunate than the cattle baron who came to Yuma with his own commitment papers. While Jack was out hunting game in the mountains one week, a citizen was murdered back home. The sheriff's officers started a search and soon found Jack Swilling.

"Who are you and what are you doing here?" they demanded.

"That's my business." Jack was always impudent. "Who are you?"

"Officers, looking for the man who killed W. T. Colley. Have you any idea who done it?"

"Why, hell yes!" Jack shot back. "Killed him myself. How do you like that?"

197

More astute officers would have known Jack was lying. He had a reputation for drinking and popping off. But these men arrested him and imprisoned him temporarily at Yuma as the only available place.

Jack Swilling is the patron saint of Arizona's Valley of the Sun, because he built the white men's first irrigation canal there, opening a vast region of agricultural wealth. But even so, Jack died in prison—awaiting trial for a murder he did not commit. Proof of his innocence came soon after his death in a Yuma cell.

One day a Mexican prisoner was working outside near the river under an armed guard's watchful eye. The Mexican stopped abruptly and picked up a rock, then stared at it intently.

"*Oro, señor! Mucho oro!*"

"Gold? Lemme see it. Quick!"

No word is more exciting—or more disarming. The guard took the rock in his hand. As he stared, the prisoner snatched his gun!

The prisoner backed away into the reeds of the river. The brave guard shouted an alarm, and other guards came running; the Gatling gun spoke and dozens of rifle shots were fired. The prisoner was seen to drop into the water, but no trace of his body could be found. He was marked on the prison books as killed in an attempt to escape.

Six months later, though, that guard received a package from Mexico. It contained his stolen rifle and a saucy note of thanks!

"Swede" Rogers was the most incorrigible prisoner ever held at Yuma, officials used to say. On one occasion Swede stayed in the snake den (a solitary dark cell) for eighty days and lived on one glass of water and three slices of bread a day. He was so weak that they had to carry him out, but he still wouldn't obey the warden. The warden let him have his way then.

Swede was a graduate of Oxford, spoke five languages, wrote excellent essays, and played a violin with concert skill. One day a women's club in Yuma asked that Swede be sent to its meeting to play for them. The warden agreed —but Swede refused to go either in stripes or under guard. Everybody argued. Finally the warden gave in again, hoping privately that Swede would manage to escape and thus rid the prison of its worst nuisance. However, Swede dressed like the scholar he was, played and spoke with great dignity, and returned to prison alone.

But one day the Swede did strike. After carefully organizing a plan to set all the prisoners free, he gave the signal and the break was begun. Commander Swede had specified one thing—no guard should be injured. Overpowered, yes; but not hurt. But immediately after the break began a convict stabbed a guard with a knife. At once Swede deserted the prisoners and joined the guards. Fighting like fury, he helped quell the break he had organized. He criticized the men bitterly for not obeying his instructions; then he went back to his own cell. For that act Swede was pardoned a month later. He dressed with meticulous care, walked haughtily out of prison, and boarded a train, and to this day nobody in Arizona has heard of him again.

Construction of Yuma Prison was authorized by the Arizona Territorial Assembly as early as February, 1875, and the site hadn't even been selected when the first prisoner arrived. He was William H. Hall, a "lifer" who came to Yuma handcuffed to officer Joe Phy.

"How come they ain't no buildings and cells for this here convict?" Mr. Phy demanded.

"Politics," a Yuma citizen answered. "It takes time, Joe, to build anything. Take him on back north som'ers."

"I won't do it. I had orders to leave him here and I'm a gonna."

Whereupon Hall, a lifer, was promptly set free in Yuma!

The news got around quickly. Hall doubtless figured to make tracks to eternal safety, but when he tried it nobody would help him. And a man cannot brave the desert sand dunes without help or equipment. For a while he was free as a deer but unable to run. Nobody would feed him or house him; nobody wanted anything to do with a convict, especially one convicted from a county two hundred miles away.

Finally, in desperation, Hall begged to be taken in at the Yuma County jail, and the sheriff took pity on him. Months later he was duly transferred to the new prison, where he belonged. Construction had been finished by then. But that still didn't settle Mr. Hall. In a short time he did escape! Somehow—the records never have been clear on it—he got across the desert. But in a distant county he committed another crime, was rearrested, retried, and resentenced to Yuma for "life."

Once more Fate played with Hall. She got him pardoned after a few years, and he walked out free. In a short time he committed a third crime, was tried, convicted, and sent back to Yuma. It was getting to be monotonous, the warden said. But Hall served that third session out and disappeared forever. Quite incidentally—and in thorough keeping with the bizarre history of the southwestern border—Mr. Phy, who first brought Hall to Yuma, was shot to death in a pistol duel with another officer in 1888.

Among the more notorious criminals on Yuma's historic roster was "Buckskin Frank" Leslie. Sixty years or so ago, certain sensational New York and Chicago newspapers "played up" Leslie's crime career for many months, often dramatizing him beyond all reason. He became internationally known. As for the Southwest, however, it was more callous toward him. Only after Leslie had committed his fourteenth murder did the Arizona citizens say it was enough. Then they grabbed him and locked him in Yuma for life.

The charming Miss Pearl Hart was among the first inmates of Yuma. She must have been charming, because she had a great many male admirers. The ones she liked she "accepted" as friends and fellow operators. The others she robbed and killed. She was known as Arizona's female bandit.

Down in the rip-roaring town of Tombstone one day, an Arizona citizen thought he would play a joke on a friend. In the Tombstone *Epitaph*, the local newspaper, he had a "reader" inserted saying that one William Kinsman was soon to marry Miss May Woodman.

The next day, in a paid advertisement, Mr. Kinsman made flat denial of his engagement to Miss Woodman. The *next* day the same paper printed—free—the news that Mr. William Kinsman had been shot to death in front of the Crystal Palace Bar by Miss May Woodman. Tombstone citizens openly opined that a man shouldn't say, or even imply, that he resented being accused of friendship with a lady so attractive as Miss Woodman, much less buy an advertisement to say it. On the other hand, the citizens agreed sagely, no lady ought to up and shoot a man to death just for denying his friendship with her, and so they got her into court and sent her to Yuma Prison for three years.

Misses Woodman and Hart were both given private quarters in Yuma, with luxurious beds and general "easy" times. Chivalry still bestirred the men who had to punish them, even if pity seldom was a consideration in sending male prisoners there.

14

DOC AND KATE
THE FIRST STAGE ROBBERS

NEITHER Dr. Thomas D. Hodges nor his contemporary, Dutch Kate, realized they were setting a precedent for six or seven decades of crime sensation. They simply needed money and took the temptation at hand. For that they live now in western history, Doc as second only to the great Joaquín Murrieta himself.

Doc's place in the wild-west picture began to be carved one day when a courier summoned him to a saloon.

"Ezra Williams was just shot down!" the courier said. "You got to come and doctor him."

Hodges found Ezra wounded but alive. He treated the man, then sat with a dozen or so rough frontiersmen to watch him suffer.

"He's in a bad way," one gambler said. "I bet he dies."

"Fifty dollars says he don't," Dr. Hodges countered.

"Done!" The gambler looked around. "Anybody else want in this pot? Make your speeches, men."

Money was free and easy in the eighteen fifties. Pretty soon the gang had wagered a total of $14,600 one way or another on Ezra Williams' life. And then a woman entered.

She might have been the angel of mercy, the agent of decency who cussed out the rough men and gave Ezra a woman's tender care. Instead, she heard the betting, waited till it was all done then stepped forward.

"You're all shorthorn pikers," she informed them. "I'll lay ten thousand dollars the son of a —— dies before sunrise."

Doc Hodges had left and so didn't meet his challenger, but other men in this California mining community chipped in and matched her amount.

"And what might be yore name, ma'am?" some miner asked.

"None of your — business," she swore it at him, "but they call me Dutch Kate."

Ezra Williams was perverse about it. He apparently died about two o'clock in the morning, but Doc Hodges was back by then and revived him. At four o'clock Ezra "died" again. By now, the hundred-odd spectators had put Ezra on a pool table in the very center of the big saloon, right under the hanging lamp. The gamblers were all seated in chairs around him, some at small tables, others just holding their bottles in their hands. Thus Ezra's bout with the Grim Reaper was much like a prize fight, with the ring in the center and the public all around.

There would be cheering, too. When Ezra would groan, one bunch of rooters would acclaim it as a promising sign. If he coughed blood, another would shriek. All card games, dice, and other minor gambling had ceased, so that people could watch this bigger game.

At ten minutes until six o'clock—long before the sun came up—Ezra cashed in his chips. Bets were paid off. Dutch Kate went out beaming, but Doc Hodges looked glum. He couldn't spare the fifty dollars. Gambling, as a sideline to the medical practice, had already cost him too much. He now felt that he had to do something drastic.

History slips a cog there and fails to tell us precisely what he did. So far, no memoirs, no faded newspaper or diary, has explained the details. But Doc Hodges comes to light again when historians later find him safe in prison—

safe, that is, from the enemies who might be after him outside. But society was not safe from Doc himself. Doc, it de-
velops, had practiced the cross-navel draw with pistols in
order to out-shoot several men known to be henchmen of
Joaquín Murrieta. It was even said that he had had a bout
with Murrieta himself and had lost but had saved his own
life through his medical knowledge. In prison, he yearned
to get out and seek revenge on several persons who were
still alive, he said. This was in the year 1855, and the prison
was Angel Island.

To get out of Angel Island, Doc used his nimble brain.
He began to develop hollow cheeks, by sucking them in
every time a guard came near. Soon he was vomiting often,
from self-inflicted causes. He appeared wan and thin by
straining the muscles of his face, neck, and shoulders and
by arching his eyebrows. In short, he was a skilled actor.
One day when he "fainted," the warden came.

"Send him to the hospital," the warden ordered. "He's
got consumption or something."

Thus Doc left the Island and got to the mainland. He
appeared very sick indeed, even unconscious. Nurses left
him momentarily unguarded. Doc Hodges promptly got up
from his bed and walked out.

Just outside, a guard saw him and said, "Hold on there!
Aren't you—?"

Splack! One powerful fist blow from the tall doctor
flattened the guard and left him cold. Doc walked away
safely.

While planning this escape, Doc also made other plans.
He had met three worthy pals in prison—men whose aliases
were Bill White, Jim Smith, and Ned Connor. Their real
names are unknown today. White was a blood-thirsty devil,
Smith was a crack shot, and Connor was a German (who
liked his Irish alias) with a crucifix tattooed on one arm and a

reputation for using his bare hands to choke his enemies to death. With amazing audacity—the details of which would be unnecessary here—Doc Hodges pulled some political wires and enabled these three villains to escape from Angel's Island. Forthwith they formed the nucleus of his new gang. They set out at once to rob homes and men.

For quite a while they evidently had much fun. Somewhere during this period the name of Dr. Thomas D. Hodges was illegally but definitely changed to Tom Bell. Probably it was adopted solely as an alias to cover his escape from prison, but the stature of the man, and especially his flat, crooked nose, made his identity unmistakable. Moreover, he continued to function from time to time as a surgeon, did "Tom Bell."

One day it was necessary to shoot a victim whom the gang encountered on the roadway, a man rightly suspected of having a belt full of gold. German Connor cracked down and wounded the man, who fell, trembling and begging for mercy.

"Oh, keep your nerve, man!" commanded Tom Bell. "All you need is a physician. I happen to be a doctor myself."

Then to everybody's astonishment, Bell laid aside his guns, took his sharp bowie knife, skillfully extracted the bullet, tore strips from his shirt, and properly bound the injured man's wound.

"We can't leave you here or you'll die," Bell then said. "On the other hand, it will be inconvenient for us to escort you home. But isn't that a wagon I hear coming?"

It was a wagon. The driver came up, suspecting nothing out of the ordinary.

"I've just rendered ten dollars worth of professional medical service to this wounded man," explained Bell. "You can carry him safely home, but I've got to have my fee."

And have his fee he did! He took it, literally, from the

pocketbook of the teamster, then forced that incensed Samaritan to load on the injured man and cart him away!

This was just the kind of joke to Tom Bell's liking. He would risk life itself to get the laugh on society, especially on people who yearned for his arrest and death. He and his men constantly waylaid citizens and robbed them. They raided isolated homes to take whatever provisions or gold dust they could find. Within a few months, of course, the countryside was aroused, and posses sought a chance to arrest or shoot the gang.

By devious methods not unlike those of his bloody predecessor, Joaquín Murrieta, Tom Bell managed to be at two or three places at the same time. This was often a result of adroit propaganda spread by his undercover henchmen, of disguises, and of tales which he himself told to unsuspecting listeners. He enjoyed nothing better than slipping unobtrusively into some tavern or saloon and joining in the sociability there. Existing documents tell one such story about him.

Some twenty or more men were gambling and drinking and yarning in a saloon, and inevitably the conversation drifted around to the exploits of bandit Tom Bell. Quickly the interest heightened.

Nearly every man there had a true episode to tell. Some had even been victimized by this bold and elusive bandit. Curses and threats and promises of death were flying. A well-dressed, well-armed but quiet man at one side table had said little. Finally he spoke.

"They tell me," he drawled, using his Tennessee accent, "that moah than one pusson has noticed his nose. It's repo'ted to be crooked and flat."

A few nodded casually, affirming this observation. A few happened to glance at him.

Utter amazement showed on their faces. Muscles became

tense. The spokesman showed a queer, sardonic grin, a hard light in his eyes. His hands rested on his pistol handles, poised for a rapid draw.

Within thirty seconds or so it dawned on the entire crowd that here sat their man. The flat, mutilated nose—relic of some early escapade—was unmistakable, even if no one had noticed it before.

Bell cackled a short, taunting laugh. Then he arose, alert, slow, his eyes mocking, and left the room. Nobody else moved until he had sprung to his horse, and the rain of bullets that followed him down the street did no harm.

During those first months of his lawless career it did not dawn on Tom Bell, or any other outlaw, to tackle the booty that was beginning to be handled more and more by the stagecoaches. The stagecoach business was new anyway. In time it became a far-reaching enterprise, a big business that involved many millions of dollars and was fraught with danger and adventure of every sort. The spectacular development of California and her gold fields had necessitated some sort of public transportation system. This, you will remember, was even before Civil War days, long before any railroads had snaked over the Rockies or along the Pacific Coast. Travel had been by ox or mule wagon, on horseback, or in private carriage. The stagecoach was a necessary development, and because roads were poor the coaches had to be sturdy and strong.

Many of the stages were shipped around Cape Horn to California from the eastern states. These stages, mostly of the Concord type, were pretty things and were built for service, too. They implied strength, as their six or eight horses dashed with them over their routes, express messenger imposingly sitting beside the driver. It was generally known that every stage carried some wealth, sometimes well into the thousands of dollars. Absolutely no other way of shipping gold dust or money was available, and there were almost no outlying banks. And yet, strangely, the stage business was nearly a decade old before a clever outlaw thought to rob one. Even the bandits seemed awed by the stage's importance and apparent strength. Actually, each stage was usually guarded by just one man, plus whatever guns the driver and passengers might happen to be carrying.

Doc Hodges, alias Tom Bell, should have thought of it before he did, because he haunted the highways to waylay lonely travelers and take their gold. But then he was often pursued, too, and spent much time dodging about the hills. By summer of 1856 he had established a strong headquarters in a mountain fastness and had more than fifty bandits under his leadership.

For his personal pleasure, Bell had taken to going nightly to the residence of Lizzie Hood, a redheaded wench who was too old to be of help herself, but who did have a daughter or two "at service." One of these daughters became the pet mistress of Tom Bell. He was in a position to pay well, and Lizzie Hood furnished good cover for him from the law. Her place was known as the Hog Ranch House. It was not far from the Mountaineer House of the then flourishing California Stage Company, on the road between Folsom and Auburn.

In due course the holdup idea must have clicked in Bell's brain, for he quickly had every employee at the Mountaineer House in his own hire. I cannot learn whether he bribed the old workers there or drove them away to put in his own hirelings, but in either case the effect was the same. Through them he could learn accurately what was going on in stagecoach circles, what rich passengers were riding, and what heavy shipments of gold were being made.

Bell was canny enough not to conduct his robbery in a manner that would involve his own henchmen, however.

He did not plan it for the Mountaineer House, but for the California House on the Camptonville Road, twenty-five miles from Marysville. In this place Bell had kept himself unknown, but he did drift into the tavern occasionally for a drink and perhaps a bit of sociability. On the afternoon of August 12, 1856, he "happened" to be there when the stage known as Langston's Express pulled in for a brief stop and a big fellow dressed as a miner got off. The miner was tired, and he went for a drink at the bar, and then sat down for a brief rest in the quiet gambling rooms. By chance, apparently, Bell opened a conversation with him.

The miner was really Smith Sutton, Bell's chief spy.

He reported to Bell that everything was okay. Four Chinese, a Negro woman, and a few white people were on the stage, said he *and also* a box containing $100,000 in gold! Pretty soon Bell said good-bye and casually drifted away. Once out of sight, he spurred his horse to a gallop.

Down a little near-by draw he came on other horsemen concealed in bushes. They were White, Smith, Connor, and a Mexican member of his gang named Juan Fernandez, an educated fellow who was, unfortunately, likely to go off half-cocked. Bell led them around a hill, down a path already carefully studied for the purpose, and so to the roadway where they could meet the slower stage. They pulled their horses to a halt behind some brush and rocks. In five minutes the coach was coming, heralded by clatter of hoofs and by the loud gabbling of the four Chinese. Most of the other passengers were dozing and thought nothing was amiss until the chatter of the Chinese abruptly stopped.

William Dobson, express agent, first saw the bandits.

He sat by the driver, John Gear, armed with two revolvers. He noticed at once that two of the unexpected horsemen were masked.

"Stop the teams! Hold up your hands!"

The commands were loud and harsh.

John Gear held up the reins, stopping the horses. But Dobson quickly drew and fired. One bandit was knocked off his horse at once.

Passengers meantime had come to life, and a miniature battle took place. Dozens of shots were exchanged quicker than it can be told.

The Negress was instantly killed. The four Chinese, screaming and chattering, jumped from the stage and ran and after a few moments other passengers fled, so that soon only the dead or wounded were left in the stage. The wounded continued fighting bravely.

Driver Gear's right hand was shot off. Bandit Bell was wounded, but stayed mounted. When he ceased fighting, however, his henchmen got panicky and fled, he with them.

"Let it alone!" Bell commanded. "Run for your lives!"

But Juan Fernandez, angered, turned back alone to renew the attack. Dobson promptly shot him down.

Presently the stage was under way again, its gold shipment undisturbed. With Dobson driving, the coach rocked on into Marysville carrying its dead and wounded, and a day later the citizens gave a rousing banquet with Dobson as the honored hero. Immediately after the dinner a posse departed bent on a clean-up of the Tom Bell desperado gang.

Meantime, Bell had slunk off with his henchmen into the hills to nurse his wound and his disappointment over the fact that the first stagecoach holdup in western history was a flat failure. Well, not entirely a failure, he admitted the next day, after he had regained his poise. His wound was not bad, and he had, to be sure, enjoyed a good deal of fun!

The countryside promptly became inflamed at news of this attempt by Tom Bell. People had come to depend on the stagecoach. It was more important to them than they themselves had realized. Why, if banditry of this fashion became popular, the thieves might wipe out several families' fortunes in one sally. There was no other way to ship their gold dust or their gold bars to the market or to the bank. The express messenger had acted bravely, but a calm survey of the holdup attempt showed that Dobson was in reality a very lucky man. With four or five masked robbers ambushing a coach, one defender should have been killed the first thing, and of course the passengers could not be expected to be of great defensive value. In short, the people became so angry that many men dropped their daily work and joined the posses to hunt Bell and his murderers down.

"It is better," said Frank Stevens, a citizens' committee leader, "that we put a stop to this thing now, before it spreads. Murder has been done, and a stagecoach robbery attempted. We must make this a warning to outlaws everywhere."

Mr. Stevens and his listeners meant well and are to be commended for their sincerity. But they could never know what a precedent Bell had set that day. Other stages were held up after that on the same road—the first "successful" one being the queer and dramatic episode engineered by Dutch Kate. The fate of these first bandits seemed not to deter criminals, because stage robbery came to occupy a prominent part in the bloody history of every southwestern community.

And what was the fate of these pioneering stage bandits?

The chase lasted almost a year. Frank Stevens and a group of his friends made the first capture. They rounded up six of the gang, including Bill White, who was in the actual holdup.

White was yellow. He knew a noose awaited him, and he whined like a baby, pleaded, begged, and turned traitor when given the chance. He went down for mercy in the name of state's evidence, because what he had to tell was interesting and important indeed. He it was who revealed, for the first time, the innermost secret of the Tom Bell gang.

He told that the gang's talisman was a bullet marked in a peculiar way with dots and a cross.

"Every member carries one of these marked bullets in his pocket," said White. "There are nearly a hundred, some right here among you as spies. No man but Bell knows all of them. But none of us will operate with others without showing these symbols of membership first."

White produced his own bullet and showed the secret markings. The impromptu court was much interested and not a little alarmed. Evidently the Tom Bell outfit was more powerful than they had suspected; it was indeed a veritable fester in the community about them. Every man went home that night suspicious of his neighbor.

It is recorded that many a man was ambushed and his pockets searched, until some thoughtful citizen pointed out that such tactics were foolish. The talisman would have been abandoned as soon as White revealed its secret. They must look for another one. But nobody ever discovered any new secret of the gang. Two suspects under arrest were found to have identical tattoo markings on their left feet, but this was finally marked off as coincidence. Meanwhile an out-and-out hunt was being conducted without benefit of detective work and was meeting with some success.

Ned Connor was riding down the road one morning, thinking that he was safe from detection, when a citizen's committee suddenly met him. Recognition was instantaneous and mutual.

"Don't shoot, men, I'll surrender!" Ned yelled, probably hoping for a chance to dash away.

"Surrender, hell!" some spokesman shouted back, "We ain't out after prisoners!"

Ned was carelessly buried twenty feet away. A bullet had pierced his heart.

One afternoon some months after the robbery Jim Smith slipped into a village, probably to purchase needed provisions for a part of the fugitive gang. In spite of a rather crude disguise that he wore, somebody recognized him. He was not accosted at once, and by the time a group of men could arm themselves Jim had disappeared. A sort of police cordon was thrown around the village until the possemen could make a thorough search.

Smith seemed to have crawled into some hole. Several hours elapsed before an aged Mexican peon mutely smoking, drove from his outlying hut with a burro pulling a cartload of hay. He looked anything but suspicious; nevertheless, the citizens were taking no chances. A little crowd surrounded him and his cart.

"What's in that rig besides hay?" somebody demanded.

"*Nada.* Nothing, *Señor.*" The old man did indeed look innocent. But the suspicious spokesman left his own horse, stooped down, and peered up under the cart, through the cracks in the bottom. He never mentioned what, if anything, it was that he saw.

"How much your hay and cart worth, old man?" he demanded.

"Why—why, possibly—*diez y cinco pesos,* but—"

"Unhitch!" the command was abrupt.

"But *Señor,* I do not—"

"Unhitch, I said. Here's your fifteen pesos. Take your burro and git!"

The order was rough and unmistakable. Scarcely had the old peon ridden to safety before the hay was a mass of flames from a light the posseman had dropped into it. It was not a pretty picture for the next half hour or so, but alias Jim Smith of the Tom Bell gang did not bother that or any other community again. Those were hard days when the necessity arose.

Meanwhile what had become of the doctor himself, of Tom Bell the leader, during this prolonged man hunt?

He had done what many another man has done when pursued, and what all of us feel a yearning to do when danger nears. He had fled to the comfort and care of a woman. Lizzie Hood and her three daughters petted and concealed him for a while. In time, though, suspicion began to be pointed at them, and the four women themselves fled, leaving Bell to take another trail. Within a day or two the women were captured in the Tulare region, and after close questioning Lizzie told a deputy sheriff where to find the bandit leader.

On the upper reaches of the Merced River one morning a small party of volunteer possemen finally saw Bell. He sat on his horse, one leg thrown over the horn of his saddle for added comfort. He saw them, too, but he mistook them for hunters and calmly allowed them to ride right up to him.

"Howdy do, gentlemen? What luck?" he greeted them genially.

They studied him closely and were satisfied. There was no mistaking that flat nose, despite the disguise in dress and manner.

"'Pears like we are having right good luck this morning," one of the "hunters" answered him. "You're the game we're after."

A cocked rifle was pointed right at Bell. He knew at once that he had made a mistake, probably his last one. He made no attempt to fight back, but permitted himself to be disarmed and tied.

"You go for the deputy sheriff, tell him to come here for his man," the spokesman ordered one rider, "but don't be in too big a rush, cause the deputy ain't more'n three mile back."

When the rider departed, the spokesman addressed the bandit chief again.

"Bell, here is a pencil and some paper. I'll loose yore hands, but not yore feet. You got twenty minutes to write yore last say."

Bell didn't squirm about it, or pretend he didn't understand. He took the paper and started a letter to his folks back in Tennessee.

As he wrote, his captors casually threw a rope up over the limb of a sycamore, stretched it, tested it, made jokes about it, all within a few feet of the writing man.

After a while the deputy came, and the possemen apologized for the fact that Bell was not among those present.

"But here, officer, is a letter he wanted mailed, also his scalp. Near as we can figger it out, he mistook some men for hunters, and they mistook him for a bear."

Thus does the Tom Bell gang pass out of California's hectic history. The man who apparently aspired to be as notorious as Murrieta lasted less than two years, all because he bungled a new kind of job that might have netted him wealth and reputation, criminal though it was. Californians heaved sighs of relief when his death became known. "There!" said they, "This crime of robbing stages is nipped right in the bud."

Little they knew! Two years more did elapse before another outlaw tried it, because after all, an unsuccessful attempt, with the bandits all run down and killed, was a pretty good deterrent. No sensible, rational outlaw would elect to try it, people said. But then, Dutch Kate didn't have an overabundance of brains.

People took warning from Tom Bell's attempt. In the months just after his sally all stage passengers wore pistols, and the upper seats sometimes carried two or more heavily armed guards. Citizens also went to some personal pains to protect their own gold. One young woman found that she could conceal a right sizable fortune in gold dust in her brassiere. Little bags resembling sachet bags, only more ingeniously designed, were placed between and around her ample breasts, and the whole was bound up in lace and silk. In the event of robbery, it was reasoned, no man would dare search her there, because even to bandits in the nineteenth century a woman's *decolletage* was sacred ground. The efficacy of this method of hiding was proven once when the good lady happened to be staying in a hotel which was held up. Only her visible jewelry was stolen.

One sage old-timer of the region adopted the peculiarly effective system of putting two live rattlesnakes in the chest where he stored his panned gold. He put air holes in the box and expressed it to his bank by stage one day, neglecting to mention what it contained. It was duly delivered, and when the banker opened it, a panic resulted. They closed out the man's account right away, and it took nearly all he had saved to pay the bitten teller's hospital and doctor bills.

However, Dutch Kate probably paid no attention to these interesting details of current finance, even if she heard about them. Kate was a busy woman, one of the two or three first professional female gamblers in the whole West.

Kate could and did cuss like any miner. She smoked cigars, probably the first woman, aside from a few Mexican crones, who smoked in California. She guzzled liquor, and, on top of it all, she wore men's clothes.

Of course, Kate knew about Tom Bell's exploit with the stagecoach; everybody knew about that. Hence when she lost two thousand dollars at cards one night and was flat broke, she naturally thought of any means that might bring easy money. By chance she learned that a shipment of gold said to be worth about forty thousand dollars was on the stage coming from Camptonville. Kate, the gambler, took a chance.

She conducted her holdup in fine style and then completely disappeared. From the moment she backed away, holding her pistols, and ordered the stage driver to "git on down the road," not another word came from her. Nobody ever saw her or heard of her again in the region where she had long lived, and at this late date even her last name is unknown. Just Dutch Kate.

Kate stepped from ambush holding two guns and commanded the driver to halt. Astonished, he did so.

"File out, hands high!" she barked at the passengers.

They obeyed and smiled openly when they discovered the bandit was a woman. One gentleman even remarked that it would be an honor to be searched by a "lady."

"Throw down that box!" Kate commanded. She decided she wanted only the express box containing the forty thousand dollars, and the driver kicked it down. Then, rather than try to search the passengers, she made them return to their seats and ordered the driver to be gone, threatening death to any who dared draw a gun.

She got away with her box and must have been well along her escape trail before she discovered that history's second stagecoach holdup—despite its easy "success"—had also been a complete failure. The express box she so boldly stole was empty! The forty thousand dollars was in another coach.

As an added injury, the newspapers soon after proclaimed that in the purse of one of the passengers she had disdained to search was gold totaling fifteen thousand dollars.

As has been said, nobody ever saw Dutch Kate again. My theory is that the poor woman probably read the newspaper, then shot herself in pure chagrin.

15

WE REMEMBER PANCHO

NOBODY in Mexico would ever have guessed that the grubby half-Indian boy Doroteo Arango would achieve undying renown. At twelve he was homeless, eternally playing the Mexican version of cops and robbers, with himself as the robber chief. He slept under the sky, ate what he could steal, and wore only a piece of sackcloth tied around his waist. Yet he lived to be *mucho hombre* in the eyes of the Mexican people. When the robber game became real he was still the leader, and there was no limit to his energy and nerve. Good or bad—and below the border that point is controversial—he lives in memory as the only military commander ever to invade the United States of America and get away with it; indeed, he was the only man ever to lead an attacking army into our nation.

The best we know of his origin is that Doroteo slipped into the world illegitimately on October 4, 1877, near Río Grande in the state of Durango. In later years quite a few women seeking reflected glory claimed to have been his mother. But from the time he was a toddler he was largely on his own, half-starved, and half-frozen, yet somehow triumphing over the diseases and accidents that took other children of his kind in the peonage of Mexico.

At fourteen he was already a vicious leader of gangs whose robber games were more than play, for at that age he was "wanted" as a cattle rustler. Boys could steal a steer, butcher it and cook a square meal, then sell the remainder for good money—if they didn't get caught. At this time in his life, too, an adult bandit of minor achievements had won some notoriety in the back country of Mexico. His name was Francisco Villa, (pronounced Vee'-yah). Young Doroteo Arango, idolizing that bandit, took his name, though he was still generally called Pancho. When the real Villa was slain, the pseudo Villa acquired some of his reputation as well, and that pleased him.

"I am Pancho Villa!" he would announce grandly at the rural *bailles* (balls), and the *señoritas* would look on, wide-eyed with interest.

Pancho developed a mighty swagger. He stole enough clothing to be colorful, and he had an infectious smile. At age sixteen he boasted accurately that he was the father of nine children. At age eighteen he had lost count. These routine adventures did nothing to belittle him, rather did they add to his standing. By the time he was twenty Pancho Villa was a more capable, more picturesque villain than the original Villa had ever been. His youthful robber band now had abundant rifles and horses, and they left a legend of magnificence wherever they raided. They affected a certain Robin Hood character, being careful to steal from some of the less popular grandees and give the loot to charity. Before his black beard had become more than a collegiate fuzz, he was already an accomplished thief, torturer, and murderer.

Cattle rustling continued to be the safest type of thievery for the young adult Pancho, and he extended this exciting activity through most of Mexico's northern states and kept at it for about ten years. Ranch owners tried to retaliate. Don Madariago del Soto y Larias took twelve picked *vaqueros*—cowboys skilled with rope and gun—to ride

Pancho down. Pancho's band had stolen Larias cattle repeatedly, and today the rustlers' trail was plain. It led six
miles, eight, twelve, fourteen, into a canyon, with Don
Madariago resolutely at the head of his vigilantes. And then
without warning came a crackle of rifle fire, echoing off
canyon walls.

"*Alto!*" Pancho Villa shouted. "*Manos arriba!*"

The good don and his men halted—indeed, four of them
had been slain in that first ambush—but they did not throw
up their hands as ordered. They tried to fight back valiantly. Only when all were down or killed did the fighting end.
Pancho's men picked up three wounded, including the don,
and carried them to camp.

"So, you come for the great Francisco Villa, eh?" Villa
taunted him. "Is good you come. We need the entertainment."

The entertainment, Villa style, was to tie Don Madariago's legs to one skittery horse and his arms to another and

turn both animals free with a whiplash to start them. They plunged off down the canyon, while Villa's bandit band howled in glee.

That could be a mere legend, a bit of anti-Villa propaganda, except for the testimony of men who saw it, Villa's own proud boasting, and the fact that it became his favorite form of torture. He especially loved to catch helpless Chinese, of whom Mexico then had some thousands, and after robbing them tie them between two horses that way. In short, by the time Villa was thirty he was the most ruthless butcherer ever to adorn that stage for melodramatic action that we call Old Mexico.

The cattle rustling soon became so flagrant that President Porfirio Díaz of Mexico issued a manifesto against him. This action brought Pancho Villa into politics. Calling himself a hero and a martyr and finding that many believed him, he became a "Mexican general," his band of unspeakable ruffians an "army." His peculiar flair for showmanship, his undeniable good looks, and his openhanded generosity toward the poor in countless little back-country villages made him something of a popular saint. He would ride up the street of a humble farming community tossing golden coins to children. He would go into a church, pray, or pretend to pray, and leave a leather bag of gold on the altar. These tricks served him better than any press agent might have done.

When our American reporters learned of him, they built his legend exactly as he would have them do. Americans are always slow to believe the worst about anybody—remember how Hitler and Mussolini were "misunderstood" for years? It was so with Villa in Mexico. He became a storybook hero, a swashbuckling knight of our time, an individual adventurer in whom every American man found something to admire. Americans did not know, then, about the tortures and the killings—and about his unconscionable mania for rape and rapine.

"The women? Ha-a-a-a-a, is fun to make a game of them, like chasing the scared rabbit or the deer!"

This was his open boast. It was easy enough just to buy a woman in Mexico, or in America, for that matter. He might easily "conquer" one at will by his virile looks and manner, for when he wished to he could turn on considerable charm, and any general of any army is a man of prestige. But General Villa's women, who in time totaled hundreds, were more often literally run down and taken by force. This unspeakable habit ultimately caused his downfall.

With President Díaz opposed to him, Villa perforce was a revolutionist, an *insurrecto*. He was quick to join Francisco Madero in that leader's rebellion against Díaz in 1910, but was captured by the Díaz general, Victoriano Huerta. Villa should have been summarily executed and probably would have been, except that a friend among the soldiers guarding him helped him escape to Texas. Nor did the United States government help recapture him. Americans were obviously thrilled that one of the real, live, genuine Mexican generals, one of the leading men in the drama of that era in Mexico, had actually come seeking refuge. They looked upon him with a certain smiling benevolence, as if he were a quaint General So-and-So in a Gilbert and Sullivan operetta. But when Huerta himself seized the presidency of Mexico, and Huerta's enemy Venustiano Carranza went into revolt, Pancho Villa went home of his own accord. He saw a chance to get rich again by joining Carranza, whose technique in politics was merely to ride, pillage, and kill.

It was then that Pancho Villa learned the first rule of his kind of warfare: loyalty can be assured only at the point of a gun. When Carranza became president, he spurned Villa. "He is a bandit and nothing else!" President Carranza shouted. "He is not for the peace of our great nation."

Villa sent a general order to all his followers: "Entrain at once. Commandeer every train, every pack animal, every man in sight, everything you need. Kill any who oppose us. We go direct to Mexico City."

He did precisely that. While the rest of the world watched, appalled by his audacity, he stormed the Mexican capital, took it, and drove President Carranza toward Vera Cruz. The Mexican populace was wild. *"Viva Villa!"* became the watchword of the hour, a slogan comparable to the "Heil Hitler!" in Germany a few years ago. For here was a "man of the people," a Robin Hood who wore a broad sombrero with gold braid on it, who carried a gleaming sword, who flung his colorful serape with just the right dramatic flourish. While sane, respectable Mexican families fled for their lives, the ignorant and the unthinking ones cheered him at every turn. And in America, the citizens too cheered. Their hero—their "Mexican General" who was just a little comic from a safe vantage point—had triumphed in a big way. They went around town talking about it and making wisecracks. "Viva Villa!" in gringo-land had a happy meaning all its own.

Meantime, events moved swiftly in the Latin land. Pancho and his men went on one prolonged splurge of plundering and dissolution. No property was inviolate, no woman safe. Pancho actually "married" seventeen girls in seventeen nights—his own boast, too sadly true. Each dawn he would tie a handful of gold in the girl's *rebozo* and literally throw her into the streets, thus divorcing her to make room for the next. He and his henchmen would see a pretty maiden, run her down on horse or afoot, tear into her home, and attack her with gleeful howlings. Whoever interfered was instantly killed. But Pancho took one too many. He tied one girl's father to a chair, attacked the girl in his presence, then threw her nude into the street. It turned out that she was a French citizen, and the French government turned its full diplomatic force onto Pancho Villa. In time this opposition mustered enough power to drive the mad *bandito* out of Mexico City.

Nevertheless, while Pancho the "Great" was thus sacking and raping his own country, President Woodrow Wilson and Secretary of State William Jennings Bryan announced that "he is the man to tie to." With an army of fourteen thousand ragged Mexicans and Indians, and six American machine gunners, he became the fair-haired boy of the western hemisphere. Later, when Villa finally had to flee to northern Mexico again, the United States did officially recognize the Carranza government. And that so angered Pancho that he hated all gringos forever after. His hatred took the form of many ruthless murders and a daring sally on March 9, 1916.

On that day the citizens of Columbus, New Mexico, suddenly heard the shoutings of the only army ever to invade United States soil. Villa roared in, accompanied, strangely enough, by American journalists, whom he pretended to like individually, and "conquered" the town. The United States had no armed force there, beyond what guns the citizenry happened to possess. Sixteen American citizens were slain, others were wounded, and half the town was burned.

At that moment "General" Pancho Villa ceased to be quaint in American eyes. Americans forgot his comic-opera aspects and at last saw him for the base villain he was. In their indignation they sent General Pershing to get him— and we would love to forget that. Pancho had darted back across the line and fled deep into the Mexican hills. President Carranza, whose support the United States had expected, stated that Pershing was leading an invading army and would be resisted by Mexican soldiers if he was not recalled at once.

225

He was recalled. And so Pancho roared on, laughing at the gringos, himself a greater hero than ever in the Mexicans' eyes. He will always be a living hero there, even though on July 20, 1923, enemies sprayed his automobile with bullets and killed him.

"We remember Pancho," the smiling courteous peons of Mexico will tell you when you go there now. "He was afraid of nobody. Not of *el presidente* in Mexico City. Not of *los gringos* to the north. Ah, that Pancho he was *mucho hombre, seguro sí!*"

16

O PIONEERS

FOR YEARS Felix Gonzales had been a short-card gambler, a drunkard, a cattle rustler, a pariah in the frontier village where he lived. But he had one moment of glory so great that even the murderous Apache Indians paid tribute to him. He was driving his wife and three children from their ranch one day in the eighteen seventies, when forty Apaches tried an ambush. Felix raced his buckboard, shooting as he drove, and the savages gave chase. At a place called The Gap, where the road squeezed between two rock cliffs, he kissed his wife quickly and said farewells.

"I've got sixteen cartridges left," said he. "You drive on to town. I'll drop out and close this Gap for you."

She whipped the horses desperately and within the hour sent back help. Outside the Gap they found fourteen dead Indians; the others had fled, but only after pausing long enough to salute a courageous paleface. They had laid out his body as if for Christian burial, instead of mutilating it as was their custom. They had left his rifle beside him, with its two unfired shells. They had even covered his face with a bandana, weighting down the corners with stones.

THE FAMOUS clothing tree used in pioneer days in Phoenix, Arizona, may have to be reinstated as tourist travel increases. A resort hotel there recently invited Maricopa and Pima Indians to a festival, saying, "Be sure to come in your native costumes." Twelve appeared—wearing nothing but narrow G strings!

As early as 1879 such handsome red nakedness became an affront to puritans, who passed a law. Nevertheless, the same whites wanted the Indians' trade in stores. To solve the problem they chose a large mesquite tree at the edge of the settlement, where the Phoenix Country Club is today, hung thereon castoff but usable clothing, then ordered the Indians to dress there as they approached town and undress again on leaving.

It worked to perfection. The reds accepted trousers and brassieres as a serious ritual comparable to their own religious rites. The tree served thus for almost twenty years.

CHUCKLING Charlie Poston would have loved the modern sequel to a little coup he staged in the Southwest almost a century ago. Charlie was a dictator, and as a result modern folk along the Mexican border still appear every few months in church or civil court distressed about their grandparents.

"*Favor*," begged one humble citizen, Señor Fabian Muñoz de la Velarde y Sáenz, "to say the words that make all of us the much legal."

He had come before a justice of the peace with his wife and eleven children. Fortunately the justice knew about Charlie Poston. Unsmiling tact is required from priest and magistrate alike, who frequently are asked for help "to clear up our family name." The justice read sonorously from a book of law, quoted a biblical passage, shook hands all around, and sent the family away happy. No fees are ever accepted, and the ceremony is entirely solemn; modern officials don't want anything to bound upon them as it bounded upon Charlie Poston.

Fortunately we have that gentleman's handwritten record of what started it all. It is a rare bit of social history. Poston was a frontiersman, now called the Father of Arizona, who went to the old adobe town of Tubac, where six Americans and about five hundred Mexicans lived, and there set himself up as a kind of super-alcalde. In 1858 he wrote this delightful confession:

"There was no priest nearer than Altar, and you know that love-making proceeds as merrily in the wildest desert as in the most romantic vale. Though self-appointed as head of the civil government, I proceeded to exercise magisterial functions and formally wedded all couples who presented themselves. This proceeding became popular, for I charged no fee and gave each bride a five-dollar dot. So all was merry, and among the dozens of almost naked urchins that played on the thoroughfares of the little pueblo many had been named or renamed in honor of me.

"Later there came the reaction. I had intruded my American ideas into Mexican customs and had to stand the consequences. I was met with scowls and curses instead of smiles. A priest had arrived, and learned of the matrimonial peculiarities of the town and immediately had excommunicated the whole bunch from the church. The women particularly were wild.

"I squared it, though it cost me about five hundred dollars. I had the priest remarry them and topped it all with a holiday and a grand *baile* (dance festival) in honor of the happy brides and grooms, not excluding their children."

Today, descendants of those good citizens are not sure how complete Poston's "squaring" was. They have only word-of-mouth history, which has in many cases grown out of its true proportions; and sometimes they learn a shocking fact about their family.

Fabian Muñoz de la Velarde y Sáenz, for example, had just learned that his great-grandmother unfortunately was absent from the remarrying ceremony which Poston arranged.

For many years prior to 1899, life in the frontier county of Navaho, Arizona Territory, had lacked excitement and fun. Therefore, at the county's first legal execution, Sheriff F. J. Wattron issued gilt-bordered invitations: "You are cordially invited to the execution of George Smiley, murderer, on December 9 at Holbrook. The latest improved methods in the art of scientific strangulation will be employed and everything possible will be done to make the surroundings cheerful and the execution a success." Decorations, music, dancing, liquor—in short, a general carnival atmosphere—were to be provided.

But Governor Murphy of the Territory, an appointed official, failed to understand the frontier mind. He reprimanded the sheriff and granted the prisoner a month's reprieve. New invitations from the sheriff then read: "With feelings of profound sorrow and regret, I hereby invite you to attend and witness the private and humane execution of a human being. You are expected to deport yourself in a respectable manner, and any flippancy or unseemly language or conduct on your part will not be allowed."

That appeased the honorable Governor. But on January 9 the whole *fiesta* was held exactly as originally scheduled, merrymaking included.

Nothing was too good for their Territory when guntotin' Arizonans were offered a new railroad in 1883. They authorized bonds, gave the money to builders, and began preparing for a celebration. But the celebration has never been held. There is no railroad to show for the money authorized, and there never has been!

One must understand that those were swift and busy

230

times. Gold, silver, and copper were being discovered throughout the Southwest; thus population was fluid. Bonds for that railroad were voted in Tucson, but in a matter of months the people who voted them, and the people who bought them, had moved on to some other boom area. So had the men who received the money. At the time, nobody was sufficiently interested to do any adequate checking up. Newspapers made an inquiring thrust or so, but nothing came of it. A few loads of crossties were hauled to the right of way, and some actual grading was done. These kept up a front of activity for a while. But in time the matter was dropped and forgotten. Not even government offices kept any record of the railroad promoters or of any efforts to supervise them.

The bonds, which, with accrued interest, totaled $868,-805.82, were to be due and payable in 1953. Arizona has no sinking fund or any hope of one with which to pay them. Nobody wants now to pay for a phantom railway! But the courts have ruled the bonds completely legal.

Therefore, don't be surprised if the sons of the Arizona pioneers resort to a little more gun totin' when the bond showdown comes.

IT WAS SAID of Luther Rodgers that he could bend a horse-shoe double with his fingers and that in a fit of anger he once killed a horse with a blow from his fist. He weighed well over two hundred pounds, and soon after he opened his blacksmith shop at the Santa Rita mines he was recognized as the strong man of the territory.

Such recognition amounted to an honor in the West in 1861, because that was an era when men were often tough and terrifying. Violence was a part of the business of living; fighting was so essential and inevitable that most men augmented their usually notable physical strength with firearms. There were murderous Indians and criminal whites, and the only law was that emanating from force alone. For most citizens the rifle was the jury and the pistol was the judge.

Not so for Luther Rodgers. He disdained the help of firearms. Oh, in an attack by whooping Apaches, he might join in the defense with guns; but for his own personal satisfaction and protection in everyday life, he relied on his fists alone. He announced that fact on the very afternoon when he first drove into the mining camp and dared anybody to dispute it.

"You figger you are right bullish with yore muscles, eh, stranger?" one miner drawled.

Rodgers' black eyes appraised the other man fiercely.

"I got bulldog in my shoulders and stud horse in my groins!" he roared, and set about to prove it.

They say that his challenger suffered concussion and was at death's door for nearly a week. Word got around that it wouldn't do to pick a fist quarrel with the new blacksmith, and the man's reputation served as advertising for him, because customers came to his shop at once, ostensibly to seek his services, but at least partly to get a good eyeful of this ferocious man.

Reference to his iron muscles, however, did not satisfy Luther Rodgers' grand ego. His boasting became twofold. He was as proud of his sexual potency as of his physical strength.

Now, a man can respect another man who brags of his muscular prowess and has the stuff to back it up. Out of fear or admiration he can accept him in his community and let him alone. He can even grin and tolerate this muscular being when he brags of his procreative powers, secure in the belief that his pride is justifiable.

But if his woman begins to show a preference for the

other, that's another matter! Among the loose women of this frontier camp the news spread that "here, at last, was a real man." They joined in considerable salacious razzing of their old and steady customers, thereby fanning a dangerous spark that has lurked in male breasts since the Paleozoic Age.

The swath that Rodgers cut in early southwestern history was a bloody one, and certainly he was one of the queerest desperadoes of all time. He was not a "bad man" in the usual sense. He didn't go around robbing and shooting up the towns. He probably never held up a stagecoach in his whole career. He wouldn't have wanted a bar of bullion that he might have stolen from the mines as other outlaws did. He was content to labor twelve and fourteen hours a day as a blacksmith—the hardest kind of work a man can do—and keep at it for months at a time.

But after a stretch of hard labor he would close up his shop abruptly and go on one hell-bustin' spree. He might disappear for a time, or he might stay around his home community.

It was during these sprees that he did his most obnoxious boasting. One Sunday morning he thundered out that he had "accommodated" twelve women the night before!

"He musta not been very partic'lar about what wimmen he chose," one old-timer relates, "becus th' husband of one of them, name of Willie McGovern, rid in to the stores for to kill him.

" 'Rodgers,' this McGovern shouted, 'I aim to cut yore— off, if it's th' last thing I do!'

"Waal, he was not no coward, was this man, but he was careless. He done some shootin' and hit Rodgers oncet, but in th' end th' big blacksmith made mush of him. He broke McGovern all up, fought like no wildcat I ever see, and ended by cuttin' off one of th' dead man's ears!'"

They didn't punish Rodgers for murder, because he had acted in obvious self-defense and because there was no law save a spontaneous one, anyway. The community did condemn him for mutilating his victim's body; after all, said the citizens, there was no excuse for cutting off an ear, even if the man had attacked you with a gun first. They sent an indignant committee to Rodgers about it.

The big fellow received them, guffawed loudly at their protest, then made an amazing confession.

"Haw haw haw!" he thundered. "So you all ain't got no use for ears, hunh? Waal, seems like to me they're right purty. Look at this'n."

He pulled the fresh one from his pocket and exhibited it. The committeemen reiterated their disapproval and their contempt and began to make it clear that such practice was frowned upon even in that free-and-easy era. But big Rodgers just laughed again.

"Why gentle-men!" He began in a peculiarly sarcastic tone. "You don't want to get excited none about one ear. I have been out in this west country a considerable spell of time and all told I have killed eighteen men! I ain't countin' in no greasers and redskins!"

Eighteen men! The committeemen looked aghast. They didn't believe him, nor did their fellow townsmen. Luther Rodgers was a notorious braggart. He would pop off at the mouth about his strong arms or his women whenever he could get an audience, and now here he was bragging about all the men he claimed to have killed. They frankly said they thought he was lying.

"Lying, hah?" the big smithy roared like a bull. "You don't believe it, hah? Didn't believe me when I claimed McGovern's ear was just one of my string. You wait!"

He stalked away to his cabin and presently returned. From his coat pocket he pulled a most amazing thing.

"Count 'em! Count 'em! See if I'm lying!"

There on a string, like some fiend's necklace, were eighteen human ears.

One of them was "green"—fresher and smellier than the others. The crowd pressed nearer, spellbound. No word was spoken, save a muttered oath or two. They stared at Rodgers in new awe.

"Waal, ain't there eighteen? You don't need to be so skittish about 'em. Some of you have tuk scalps. I don't go in for scalps none. Too messy. Cain't see where ears is no worse."

One fellow addressed him, sputtering.

"B-but, but these here are *white* ears!"

"Yair, eighteen of 'em. And lemme tell you something —" Here the huge blacksmith leaned over confidentially and spoke ominously like an ogre from some nether realm, "I'm goin' to make that necklace twenty-five ears before I'm done! *Twenty-five, do you hear me?*"

How was he to get them? Was he to sneak around over a period of years, pick his fights and add to his collection one by one? Or was he destined to go on a single grand, insane, murderous spree and get them all at once?

Apparently destiny chose the latter course for him—arranged first for him to get all seven of his ears in one bloody hour—but at the last moment diabolically changed the plan so that he got only six. Unseen fate does, sometimes, step in with just such rare, dramatic skill.

He got the six. At El Paso he fell out with a family, used an axe, a club, and doubtless his fists to end six lives. No one can say whether his motive was robbery or revenge or just plain craziness. Most persons thought the fellow was insane. At any rate that brought the total to twenty-four ears.

So horrible a crime, of course, could not go unnoticed, no matter what the cause, and in due course Luther Rodgers, the strong man who had bulldog in his shoulders and stud horse in his groins, was walking, pale and fearful, down a street in the custody of a muttering throng.

They did not hang him.

They suspended him, heels up, over a pile of brush and fagots to which they touched a torch. No doubt fiendish devils danced around this bonfire of justice, gleeful in the knowledge that Rodgers' own ears made the twenty-fifth pair.

WHILE YOUNGER generations forgot old wars and feelings, two elderly but fierce characters in the Southwest maintained the frontier antagonism between whites and Indians right down to 1947.

One was Ed Cummings, a guide at the Grand Canyon. The other was Chief Watahomigie of the Havasupai, tribesmen who live down on the Canyon floor. Over sixty years the enmity of the two men found expression in cupidity, each for the other's one most prized possession. As early as 1888, it is said, Ed swore he'd get the chief's fine hand-tooled saddle. At the same moment, Watahomigie told the Canyon gods and all mortals that one day he would own Ed's beautiful hand-wrought silver spurs.

Their feud has colored the legend of the vast Canyon country. Each man was a trifle arrogant, yet somehow magnificent in his racial pride, strong and courageous as the great ponderosa pines that defy the Canyon winds. Each had a following, hence many bets were placed, much advice was given, and many little side arguments were heard. But no amount of trickery, money, or pressure of any kind during the six decades ever enabled Ed to get that saddle or the Chief to get his spurs.

The feud finally ended on February 16, 1947, when

236

Chief Watahomigie suddenly died. Whites and reds alike gathered at the Canyon cemetery to honor him—and at the moment when the first shovel of earth was to be turned back into the grave, Ed Cummings came out of the forest and dropped in his silver spurs.

F   Arnold, Oren.
786   Thunder in the Southwest; echoes from the
A75t   wild frontier. With drawings by Nick Eggenhofer.
       [1st ed.]   Norman, University of Oklahoma
       Press [1952]
         237p. illus. 23cm.

340702

1.Frontier and pioneer life-Southwest, New. 2.Southwest,
New-History. I.Title.